Apostolic Technologies

Supernatural Algorithms

David Stafford

ISBN 979-8-88685-671-2 (paperback)
ISBN 979-8-88685-672-9 (digital)

Christian Faith Publishing
832 Park Avenue
Meadville, PA 16335
www.christianfaithpublishing.com

Unless otherwise indicated, all scripture quotations are from the Holy Bible Authorized King James Version.

Printed in the United States of America

In memory of Evangelist Melvin L. Smith Sr. who through impartation activated my calling into ministry. Melvin had a clear apostolic calling on his life. He was an early pioneer of the deliverance ministry and a true sent one. In October of 1987, while leaving his hotel on his way to minister at a church in Colorado, Melvin was martyred in the parking lot by an assassin's rifle bullet. Though I miss him, I know I will see him again in the coming Kingdom.

*Now I want you to know, brothers, that what has happened
to me has really served to advance the gospel.*
—Philippians 1:12 NIV

Contents

Foreword

My friend and co-laborer, Apostle David Stafford, is a man of prayer, faith, and integrity. We've been in covenant relationship for over thirty years. I first encountered David when he came to Crusaders Deliverance Ministries to learn and study deliverance. Being a humble young man, David was evangelizing souls in Chicago and entreated me to come minister to the people God was using him to reach. They needed deliverance and spiritual training, and he was in the learning process himself. We began to be invited to minister as a team in other churches in the Chicago land area, casting out demons and healing the sick. I had a little saying, "If Buford doesn't get them, Stafford would" when it came to casting out demons and advancing the Kingdom of God.

Over the years, I have observed the precise and excellent manner David labored and shared the Word of God. He has even helped me in editing and writing several manuscripts.

After reading *Apostolic Technologies*, I am honored to recommend that everyone will benefit from the apostolic content of this book, saint and sinner. The first part of this book is written painstakingly, meticulously, lovingly as a training manual/textbook. If you are looking for fluffy and fill-in words, you won't find any. Ephesians 2:20 says, "And are built upon the foundation of the apostles and prophets, Jesus Christ himself being the chief corner stone." Second Timothy 2:15 admonishes us to "study to show thyself approved unto God a workman that needeth not to be ashamed, rightly dividing the word of truth." The foundational teachings in the first part of this book will prepare any sinner, new believer, and seasoned saint to walk in confidence in the Kingdom of God. Take time and read how to make sure your spiritual foundation is sure.

APOSTOLIC TECHNOLOGIES

The second half of *Apostolic Technologies* exposes you to more of Apostle David Stafford's maturity and years of wisdom and experience in applying new apostolic technologies in this new era. This is a timely and prophetic application of new systems and adjustments that must be made in order to help the Church advance the Kingdom of God. There is a practical "how to" become an effective kingdom citizen written upon the pages of this book. God has anointed the pages of this book; may revelations of His Word be engrafted into you that are able to save your soul. The last pages of *Apostolic Technologies* teach you how to engage one of your most powerful weapons in your warfare arsenal: fasting. I celebrate and congratulate Apostle David Stafford on completing this gift to the Body of Christ.

In His Service,
Apostle Albert Buford Global Apostolic
Prophetic International Ministries
Senior Pastor of New Heart Worship Center International

Apostle David Stafford has truly received divine revelation concerning God's supernatural algorithms, giving biblical insight to the church and nations of the world.

I met Apostle David Stafford in the early 1990s while attending Crusaders Church in Chicago, Illinois, under the leadership of Apostle John Eckhardt.

David is an anointed foundational instructor educating the people of God in the doctrine of Jesus Christ (Hebrews 6:1–7). His teaching and studying skills amplify the learning process and will dramatically increase the wisdom and knowledge gained from reading the Bible. "Take fast hold of instruction; let her not go: keep her; for she is thy life" (Proverbs 4:13 KJV). David's hallmark motto is "Do the Word" (James 1:22).

As I launched into full-time ministry—Christ In You, Hope of Glory Ministry—David came aboard as my associate pastor, assisting me in the work that God called me to do. While under my administration, he was ordained and released as an apostle to do apostolic missionary work on the continent of Africa.

This book is loaded with vital information and is highly recommended. It will enhance your study skills. I'm grateful for the privilege of reading it.

Apostle Calvin Smith
Senior Pastor
Christ In You, Hope of Glory Ministry

Apostolic Technologies Supernatural Algorithms is a book every minister should study. It is truly a cutting-edge present truth revelation from the heart and mind of God. Many other apostles and prophets will glean from the contents of this book. As a major promoter of the apostolic, prophetic, and deliverance ministries, I can truly recommend this book as being a vital contribution to what God is doing within His Church.

Dr. Apostle Ivory Hopkins
The General of Deliverance
Founder and Overseer of Pilgrims Ministry of
Deliverance in Georgetown, Delaware

Introduction

God Is a Technological God

> *Talk no more so exceeding proudly; let not arrogancy*
> *come out of your mouth: for the* LORD *is a God of*
> *knowledge, and by him actions are weighed.*
>
> —1 Samuel 2:3

The name LORD used in the above scripture is Yehovah, the self-existent or eternal Yehovah, the Jewish national name of God. The name GOD is "El," meaning strength; the Almighty. From this scripture, we can conclude that the self-existent, eternal Yehovah is the Almighty of knowledge. In the natural realm, knowledge stimulates technology. From the broom to the vacuum, wax paper to ziplock plastic, toaster ovens to microwaves, typewriters to word processers, and landline telephones to handheld, wireless video cell phones, all technology evolves from newly discovered scientific knowledge. Our God has all knowledge, and he is a technological God. "He is the God of all technology." He has preprogrammed every past technology and algorithm—all that presently exists and those that will be discovered in the future. Science has been and still is today on the path of discovering these technologies.

So what exactly is technology? Technology is the practical application of knowledge especially in a particular area. A capability given by the practical application of knowledge, it is a manner of accomplishing a task especially using technical processes, methods, or knowledge. Note, that when it comes to technology, the operative word is knowledge. Someone once said, "I don't understand how electricity works, but I am not going to sit in the dark until I do!" In other words, we do not have to understand the physics behind the movement of charged particles to benefit from the use of electricity. Children do not always know what is best for them; however, a parent can give step-by-step systematic directives that when obeyed and acted on will produce the desired results, even though the child, because of their immaturity, lacks the ability to comprehend the scope or nature of the issue at hand; that is how an algorithm operates. An algorithm is a precise step-by-step systematic plan for a computational procedure that begins with an input value and yields an output value in a finite number of steps. It is a precise rule (or set of rules) specifying how to solve some problem. Algorithms are all around us, and without our knowledge, we use them in our day-to-day lives; from buying groceries in the supermarket to telephone answering systems, or paying bills by an automated service. Algorithms are intrinsic to technology and have become an integral part of our lives.

Algorithms seemly give life to inanimate objects or computer systems, allowing us to talk and interact with them by a technology called VRT or voice recognition technology. Algorithms are the building blocks of computer programming that make the automation of mechanical machinery possible. Algorithms contain what I call "procedural knowledge."

Modern-day technology leaders Microsoft, Intel, Monsanto, Boeing, IBM, and AT&T have used technology to affect all of society; how we travel, how we view the world, how we communicate. In doing so, they have amassed fortunes. This new form of technocracy is subtle yet bold, integrating itself in to every facet of social order, happening almost without our awareness yet aggressively shaping culture on a global scale. Today, procedural knowledge integrates technology, enhancing its ability and functionality. Seemingly by comparison, it is simple to surmise that this natural application of knowledge and methodical wisdom is not parent in origin but rather the offspring of a more bona fide, authentic spiritual realm. The God kind of wisdom is the ability to make sensible decisions based on knowledge. In other words, God's wisdom is the practical life-giving application of knowledge (Ecclesiastes 7:12). This knowledge and wisdom are companions and have always been eternally resident in the Almighty. If the technology moguls of our day were called to compete with the Lord, they would come up pitifully short, because when it comes to wisdom and knowledge, the LORD GOD is technologically savvy.

> O the depth of the riches both of the wisdom and knowledge of God! How unsearchable are his judgments, and his ways past finding out! For who hath known the mind of the Lord? Or who hath been his counsellor? Or who hath first given to him, and it shall be recompensed unto him again? For of him, and through him, and to him, are all things: to whom be glory forever. Amen. (Romans 11:33–36)

No one can match the knowledge of God or the depth of his wisdom; he is omniscient, all-knowing. God has all knowledge and wisdom. He knows all about all; he is God. Science, as I said, has always been on the path of discovery. These discoveries center around natural science technology of which God is Lord (spiritual technologies exist also and are the main focus of this book). In this realm of natural science, it is the discovery of what is called "new technologies" that bring breakthroughs leading to advancements in medicine, communications, engineering, transportation, agricultural, etcetera. However, these are not new technologies but rather new discoveries. All the current knowledge that drives technology today existed during and prior to the time Jesus Christ walked the earth. Although man had not yet discovered this knowledge, nonetheless it existed then as it does now. Even so, there is wisdom and knowledge that will give birth to technologies of the Spirit that have yet to be tapped by the church. These spiritual technologies will not be discovered by any means of natural science but rather revelation (Matthew 16:17). It takes *revelation* knowledge to bring spiritual truth, spiritual technologies, and spiritual strategies to light. This is why the prophet and the prophetic ministry are so vital to the local church. The prophetic ministry can tap into diverse assortments of spheres in the Spirit; it is through the prophetic that the church taps into the hidden wisdom of God (1 Corinthians 2:7). All these technologies and algorithms, both natural and spiritual, predate the foundations of the world because God is an eternal, omniscient God, and all knowledge, wisdom, and understanding originates in him.

> Hast thou not known? Hast thou not heard, that the everlasting God, the LORD, the Creator of the ends of the earth, fainteth not, neither is weary? There is no searching of his understanding. (Isaiah 40:28)

God is Lord over all science, having authored the various algorithms, laws, and technologies that govern its very existence. These governing laws and principals perceptible to man are taught in schools and for the most part can be experienced to some degree by the natural senses. However, the Bible teaches that the things we can see (perceive with our natural senses) were not made from the things that we see. In other words, the natural substances that we can see, feel, or contact with the natural physical senses were not originally created by natural means or substances; as paradoxical as this may seem, it is what the Bible declares. To understand this concept, it takes something more than a doctor of science degree from MIT; yet we can know by faith what we cannot comprehend with the natural mind.

> Through faith we understand that the worlds were framed by the word of God, so that things which are seen were not made of things which do appear. (Hebrews 11:3)

Natural sciences are evolutionary. A quick look back at the history of science will show that every law of science from the 1915 edition of the *Encyclopedia Britannica,* which at that time were the experts in various areas of technology, are today considered irrelevant. The earlier methods are now outdated because science evolves. Through time and discovery, it changes. There are also spiritual laws, algorithms, and technologies at work beyond the natural visibility of human perception. These forces supersede the tangible physical realm, including natural sciences and the various physical substances that exist.

The complexion of Christianity in the early nineteen hundreds is no different than it is today; and although its core has not changed, the church at large remains institutionalized, and there are some who fight to stay in the old wineskin of past generations. Songs have been written concerning this past glory with emphasis on remaining there by making declarations of its efficiency or effectiveness. Songs with lyrics like "Give me that old time religion / it's good enough for me" keep people stuck in yesterday's move of God when the cloud of God has broken camp. It is not my intent to condemn the old but merely point out the fact that it is outdated, similar to an outdated computer operating system that lacks the ability to access and interface with new and changing technologies of the day. The mindsets of the past are ill-equipped to grasp the technological global world in which we currently live. The operating system of the church must be upgraded. This is unlikely to happen under the current institutionalized pastoral mindset of the church, whose primary function is to protect and maintain. The church must have apostolic leadership that will pioneer and take risks to advance the kingdom of God over a global landscape. This is the commandment and assignment of the church (Mark 16:15).

Today, the prophetic word releases new songs and revelation giving us creative concepts of prophetic and apostolic archetypes. The Holy Spirit is calling for an upgrade of the operating system and a doing away of the old worldly structure that encapsulates the church. Although not new, they are fresh apostolic patterns for the twenty-first-century church. These fresh exemplars transform our mindset of what church is and the way we "have church." This includes music and music styles, different sounds and veins of flow where the anointing, glory, and the presence of God are released.

These new sounds and styles of music are not natural in origin but rather birthed from the Spirit. However, just a change of genre or surface renewal is not sufficient; the major shift must be away from the current worldly institutionalized structure and a return to the indigenous new creature (2 Corinthians 5:17, Galatians 6:15), the alien spiritual life form called the church (1 Corinthians 12:27). If natural science can evolve and change, then surely the realm that created them, the Spirit realm, can more so advance, yet it is not an advance; it is, in essence, a return or reformation of recovered spiritual truth.

Just as that which is natural can be upgraded by what is called current or new technologies, the twenty-first-century church, through the prophetic ministry, must tap into fresh techniques, methods, and technologies of the Spirit that have become foreign to her but were the modus operandi of the first-century church. This is not a move backward nor a move forward but rather a reformation to reestablish what has been lost and has become inoperable in the body of Christ. Perhaps it is time to rethink the church and her function. Today we can look at the church in China and see the Lord doing a profound work among the seemingly unorganized (by natural standards) "house church." Is this not scriptural? (Acts 2:46–47). The reports of the church in China are astounding, to say the least, because between a thirty-year period, from 1956 to 1986, the underground Chinese church lived under severe persecution, probably as harsh as that of any church in the world. Estimates of those killed go into the millions. In addition, virtually the entire evangelical Chinese-Christian intelligentsia was destroyed or silenced. Therefore, by even the most conservative estimates, the Chinese church must be considered one of the most victorious in the world. During a thirty-five-year period when the church in the developed countries had not experienced any significant growth at all, and in many places decreased in size, the Chinese church (church in China) grew at a rate of twenty to perhaps fiftyfold. It seems today that most of the fermentation of growth in China is occurring, not in the government-sanctioned Three-Self Patriotic Movement (TSPM) churches, but in less organized and illegal house churches.[1] Today, twenty-five years later, this growth continues. Some academics who study religious movements in China agree. Protestant Christianity especially, they say, is experiencing "explosive" and even "exponential" growth in China, both in the countryside as well as in major cities: from Heilongjiang province in the north to Guangdong province in the south, from cities like Shanghai and Chengdu, to Beijing and beyond. When Mao Zedong first took control of the country in 1949, there were just one million Christians in China. Today, while it is difficult to calculate a precise number, many now estimate that number to have grown by a hundredfold. By comparison, the Communist Party itself has just seventy million registered members, and the numbers of Christians are growing. Some academic studies place that growth at 5 to 7 percent annually. But most feel that pace has now accelerated. Today, that Christian community exceeds one hundred million and is growing rapidly. "The house churches have been growing so fast," eminent American sociologist Richard Madsen told an audience in Philadelphia, "that the government can neither stop them, nor ignore them."[2] Surely there is a technology of the Spirit at work in this church that is absent in her western institutionalized counterpart. There is a parallel lesson to learn by looking at the church in China, contrasting its growth with the western American church, and comparing it all to what transpired in Rome around AD 300. Prior to AD 300, the church at the time of the Roman Empire could not be defined by the structure that we Americans today call church. It was a church that could not be stopped by oppression or persecution. On the contrary, these forces only fueled its growth as it spread profusely throughout the known world. The first-century church multiplied and spread like a computer virus on the earth that could not be eradicated. Throughout the book of Acts, this type of spontaneous growth is seen. Under strong persecution, the church at Antioch is birthed in which we see the blueprint of this living organism under the auspices of the Holy Spirit. However, in AD 313, a subtle yet undermining mutation took place under Emperor Constantine, who many believe to be the first Christian Roman emperor. Constantine reversed the persecutions of his predecessor Diocletian and issued the Edict of Milan, which proclaimed religious tolerance of Christians throughout the empire[3]. Christianity became the state religion. On one hand, a notable Roman reform embracing Christendom causing persecution to cease; on the other hand, a subtle change that marked the beginning of the institutionalization of the church. Since that time, the veracity of this living organism has stunted into a mutative form, seemingly being genetically altered by the confinement of its wineskin called organized religion.

Although there have been many reformations since AD 313, for the most part, the church continues to embrace organizational characteristics modeling the world that are not found in the original first-century church, while religious denominations of our day fight intensely to defend the worldly structure of their organizations. The Bible commands us not to love the world or the things that are in the world (1 John 2:15). I believe this includes methods, practices, and worldly operating systems. Can we really say we have come out from the world when the very structure that encapsulates the church is patterned after the world and not the kingdom?

Could it be that because Satan could not stop the viral spread of Christianity through the world by persecution of the church that he switched his tactic from persecution and extermination to tolerance and containment? I submit to you that there is a dumbing down of the church, not of divine truth nor of nurturing relationships but of its apostolic mission; this is the DNA of church. When you tamper with an organism's DNA, you create a mutant offspring of the original organism. Institutional religion by containment has sought to reprogram the church, training and indoctrinating members to sit silently and warm the pews. This is an act of demobilization. Demobilization is the process of standing down a nation's armed forces from combat-ready status. This may be as a result of victory in war, or because a crisis has been peacefully resolved and military force will not be necessary. It is also an act of changing from a war basis to a peace basis including disbanding or discharging troops.[4] (This seems precisely what occurred in AD 313.) Has the church made peace with an institutional worldly system? Institutionalization has caused the saints to stand down, consequently deactivating the churches' apostolic mission. The mandate is to advance the kingdom of God, expand, and take dominion; this is the apostolic mindset. If the church of Jesus Christ is to be God's people doing God's will in the earth (Ephesians 4:11), then there must be a mindset shift from the ordained to ordinary, from the spectator to the participant, from a come-to to a go-to apostolic mentality. The Lord has called for a reactivation and remobilization of the body of Christ.

The architects are here; wise master builders are now coming forward to redesign an operating system for a twenty-first and twenty-second-century church. They will design, by the science of the Holy Spirit, with revelation knowledge using apostolic technologies and supernatural algorithms. It will take the pioneering anointing of the apostles working with prophets to REFORM and bring forth this new wineskin.

I am not talking about rebooting the current operating system of the church. The new wine is not compatible with the old wineskin. The redesigned operating system's architecture must be accurate, reflecting the kingdom now culture absent of the futurist mindset and worldly structure. The wineskin must be reengineered not with reheated religious theology but with authentic apostolic technologies. My prayer is that this book will be instrumental in tearing down and destroying strongholds that compose today's conventional institutionalized religious mindsets. May it release a revelatory anointing that will equip the saints and ignite strategic, spiritual technologies clearly revealing and restoring to the body of Christ her divine apostolic identity.

Today the church must get into the current river of God, the current apostolic flow of God's spirit. History shows that spiritual upgrade is revelatory and is established by the reformation of current revelation knowledge of recovered spiritual truth.

1

The First and Last Adam

And so it is written, the first man Adam was made a living soul; the last Adam was made a quickening spirit. Howbeit that was not first which is spiritual, but that which is natural; and afterward that which is spiritual. The first man is of the earth, earthy; the second man is the Lord from heaven. As is the earthy, such are they also that are earthy, and as is the heavenly, such are they also that are heavenly (1 Corinthians15:45–48).

The name Adam is more than just a name. It is the name that represents all of mankind. Adam is the name of the first man that God made, yet there are two Adams or two representatives of mankind. Scripture refers to these men as the first Adam and the last Adam; not the first and the second but the first and the last. This means that even though the last Adam was second to appear in succession to the first, he is last in the cycle of human manifestation. On the other hand, even though he is called the last Adam, he is also the first of his kind or type a first fruits breed (1 Corinthians 15:20–23). According to Romans 5:14, the first Adam was only a figure, the word *tupos* meaning "a type" (i.e., a person or thing prefiguring a future person or thing). This word also means "the image of gods."[5] Of course we understand that an image is just that—an image. Let's examine this more closely. The first man Adam was made a living soul. The making of this man is unique in origin and is recorded in the first and second chapters of Genesis.

The charge of dominion

> And God said, let us make man in our image, after our likeness: and let them have dominion over the fish of the sea, and over the fowl of the air, and over the cattle, and over all the earth, and over every creeping thing that creepeth upon the earth So God created man in his own image, in the image of God created he him; male and female created he them. And God blessed them, and God said unto them, Be fruitful, and multiply, and replenish the earth, and subdue it: and have dominion over the fish of the sea, and over the fowl of the air, and over every living thing that moveth upon the earth. (Genesis 1:26–28)

God commissioned the first man Adam to take dominion over all the earth. From this scripture, we see that this mandate is carried out in five distinctive functions that reflect the characteristics of the kingdom of which we are now a part of. Divine purpose is the foundation of this Adams rulership. Because of the authority he received from God, in a sense, Adam was the god of this world. When the first Adam sinned, he could not carry out his divine purpose or fully complete the will of God for humankind.

1. Be fruitful (Matthew 13, John 15:16, Isaiah 5:1).
2. Multiply (John 3:30, Isaiah 9:7).
3. Replenish the earth (Ephesians 1:23, Isaiah 6:7).
4. Subdue (1 John 5:4, Romans 8:37).
5. Take dominion (Matthew 16:19, 1 John 4:7).

The mandate that God gave the first man Adam reappears in New Testament objectives as God circumvents his plan to accomplish his original purpose for man in Christ.

> And the LORD God formed man of the dust of the
> ground, and breathed into his nostrils the breath
> of life; and man became a living soul. (Genesis 2:7)

According to the *Strong's Concordance*, we can see here that the first man Adam was formed a *living* the Hebrew word *chay* (2416), meaning alive raw flesh or living thing. *Soul* is the Hebrew word *nephesh* (5315), meaning a breathing creature, i.e. animal or abstract vitality. The life that this first Adam received is chay nephesh. I call this "creation life." It is life in the natural realm. Whatever God breathes on or into becomes alive with this life because God is life. So we see Adam was made in the image and likeness of God, formed from the dust of the ground, and received creation life from the mouth of God breathing into his nostrils, which caused him to become "chay nephesh"—a living soul. His scope of authority is over the fish of the sea, the birds of the air, the cattle (meaning all animals). His sphere of dominion is over all the earth and everything that creeps upon the earth. Now let us look at the word *image* in Genesis 1:26. The word *tselem* means "a phantom," (i.e., (fig.) illusion, resemblance; hence, a representative figure, especially an idol[6]). For the sake of comprehension, we could also say that the first Adam was a replica. According to the English dictionary, a replica is an accurate copy of something. A replica is also a model, facsimile, duplication, reproduction, mock-up or a carbon copy. Now a carbon copy looks like the real McCoy, but it is not; it is still only an image of the original. My point is this: even though the first Adam is made in the image of God, after his likeness and given dominion, he is still just a figure or replica. Case in point: if a man drowns and is pulled from the water not breathing and someone administered CPR and he begins to breathe again, this man does not take on the unique character and nature of the one who manually forced air into his lungs; to the contrary, the respiratory system of the resuscitated man is simply rebooted to the former state of life. Even so, God has the ability to breathe by his spirit on or into something (Numbers 22:28) or someone working a work to accomplish his will and purpose without depositing the essence of who he is.

> For he shall be great in the sight of the Lord, and shall drink neither wine nor strong drink; and he shall be filled with the Holy Ghost, even from his mother's womb. (Luke 1:15)

God did a work by his Spirit in the life of John the Baptist, prior to his physical birth; he was filled with the Holy Ghost while in his mother's womb. In Luke 7:28, Jesus said that out of all people born of a woman, there is no greater prophet than John the Baptist, but he that is least in the kingdom of God is greater than John. What does this mean? How can John be the greatest prophet born of a woman yet the least in the kingdom is greater than him? Even though John was filled with the Holy Spirit (the breath of God) in his mother's womb before his natural birth, he was not born again. Am I saying that John the Baptist was not saved? Of course not. He was justified by faith. However, what John lacked was the nature of the one who was to come after him (Matthew 3:14).

As I stated previously, God has the ability to breathe by his spirit on or into something or someone, working a work to accomplish his will and purpose without depositing the essence of who he is. God breathed into Adam's nostrils the breath of life (creation life), and man became a living soul, yet this first Adam was still only a figure, a replica, of that which was to come. This first man Adam did not possess the nature of God. He lacked the essential essence of who God is; God is holy. In other words, the first man Adam lacked deity DNA. In order for mankind (represented by Adam) to take on the nature of God, it requires something more than just the breath of God. It requires a seed.

2

The Apostolic Seed

In the garden, the serpent was able to overthrow creation life and contaminate all of humankind. Because of the first Adam's disobedience to God, sin and death entered the world. This sin nature is thus downloaded to every succeeding generation after the fall of Adam (Romans 5:12), and all bear his reproach at the time of conception.

> Behold, I was shapen in iniquity; and in sin did
> my mother conceive me. (Psalm 51:5)

This sin nature causes all of mankind to acquiesce toward disobedience to God. Disobedience causes a break in fellowship with God. The outcome of broken fellowship with the source of life can only lead to death, and so was the state of all of mankind.

> And I will put enmity between thee and the
> woman, and between thy seed and her seed; it
> shall bruise thy head, and thou shalt bruise his
> heel. (Genesis 3:15)

Soon after the fall of the first Adam in the garden, God announces judgment on the serpent and then gives a prophetic word to the serpent that is nothing short of poetic justice. The strategy that the enemy used to cause the fall of man (deceiving the weaker vessel), bringing sin and death into the world, will now be used against him. It will be the seed of the woman that will usher in his defeat. God will use the seed of the weaker vessel to destroy the serpent's power and seal his eternal doom. It will be the seed of a woman, not the seed of a man. This is an important distinction that God is making, for men have seed also, and seed is something that God takes very seriously.

> And Judah said unto Onan, Go in unto thy brother's wife, and marry her, and raise up seed to thy brother. And Onan knew that the seed should not be his; and it came to pass, when he went in unto his brother's wife, that he spilled it on the ground, lest that he should give seed to his brother. And the thing which he did displeased the LORD: wherefore he slew him also. (Genesis 38:8–10)

Onan knew that his seed was needed to impregnate his brother's wife, but for selfish reasons, he did not want to impregnate her. Rather than give his seed, he chose to throw his seed away, and God killed Onan for intentionally spilling his seed on the ground. When it comes to human reproduction, it takes the seed of a male and a female. Without which, there is no conception. In this process, the seed of the woman, the ovum, the female reproductive cell is germinated or fertilized by the semen or sperm, the male reproductive cell, the seed of the man. Let us keep in mind the prophetic word. God says that it will be the seed of the woman which will bruise (overwhelm) the serpent's head.

> And I will put enmity between thee and the woman, and between thy seed and her seed; it shall bruise thy head, and thou shalt bruise his heel. (Genesis 3:15)

The Almighty God himself begins to prophesy about a seed: "And I will put enmity between thee and the woman." The word enmity is "eybah,"[7] meaning "hostility." God is literally declaring war between the serpent's seed and the seed of the woman. It shall bruise thy head.[8] The word *ro'sh* meaning "head rank." Thou shalt bruise his heel.[9] The word `*aqeb* meaning "the rear of an army." This is a warring seed that will wage war and be victorious over the enemy. This seed has power to overwhelm and defeat Satan's hierarchy. This is a prophetic apostolic seed; a sent seed, prophetically engineered, coded, and programmed to demolish the works of the devil.

> And I will put enmity between thee and the woman, and between thy seed and her seed; it shall bruise thy head, and thou shalt bruise his heel. (Genesis 3:15)

By faith in this prophetic promise of an apostolic seed, our forefathers before the flood and the patriarchs were justified and saved. This is the messianic gospel. It is the gospel of Christ in seed form. It is the protoevangelium; it speaks of His coming in the flesh, his incarnation through the seed of a woman, and his power to deliver. This prophetic promise gave great encouragement and the blessed hope of salvation to all sinners who believed.

> For this purpose the Son of God was manifested, that he might destroy the works of the devil. (1 John 3:8b)

Natural conception algorithm

In order to procreate, a man and a woman must come together; more specifically, a man's seed must fertilize a woman's seed. Here is the basic natural conception algorithm:

Man's seed + woman's seed = conception = birth

With the understanding of this basic natural algorithm, scientists have taken this process of conception to levels once thought to be impossible. Today, medical science has not only identified the microscopic components within the human reproductive cells (genes and chromosomes) but also through a technology called in vitro insemination (in vitro is Latin for "within the glass"). Doctors successfully fertilized egg cells in petri dishes. The embryo is then implanted in the uterus of the woman. This procedure has helped many infertile married couples enjoy the blessing of parenthood. Scientists have in fact successfully cloned livestock cows, pigs, and goats for many years now. Animal cloning is the process by which an entire organism is reproduced from a single cell taken from the parent organism and in a genetically identical manner. This means the cloned animal is an exact duplicate in every way of its parent; it has the same exact DNA. Cloned beef is now in our supermarkets. Cloning is becoming a major enterprise, and perhaps without your knowledge, you may have eaten cloned beef. Cloning is gaining momentum as a major (ahem) cash cow. Scientists have been effectively cloning animals since the early 1960s, when a Chinese embryologist cloned an Asian carp. It's just a matter of time until cloned humans start emerging from test tubes; meanwhile, we natural-borns are just starting to chow down on cloned meat (which the USDA does not require producers to label)[10]. Through genetic engineering, scientists at companies like Monsanto have technology that allows them to genetically engineer corn seed, programming or activating certain desirable traits and programming out or deactivating undesirable traits, causing the seed to give maximum yield. Seeds can be coded, making the plant resistant to certain environmental conditions and parasites. This technology can be instrumental in growing crops in drought-stricken areas.

Artificial insemination

Artificial insemination, or AI, is the process by which sperm is placed into the reproductive tract of a female for the purpose of impregnating the female by using means other than sexual intercourse or NI. In humans, it is used as assisted reproductive technology using either sperm from the woman's male partner or sperm from a sperm donor[11]. The name of this technology is a bit misleading as there is nothing artificial used other than the procedure itself. This assisted reproductive technology has also helped childless married couples fulfill their dreams of having a family. It is clear to see the evolutionary scientific advancements made in recent years. Many of the accomplishments today would have been considered science fiction a few short years ago. These accomplishments are astonishing, but we should not be overly shaken by them for these are the mere feats of men. What medical science is currently able to achieve in the area of reproduction is something that God has been doing above and beyond the theater of the natural supernaturally for centuries. Throughout the Bible, we find women who could not have children, women who were barren, women who had never during their lifetime conceived, even a man and woman who both were past childbearing age, miraculously conceive and give birth by the ability and power of God.

> Who against hope believed in hope, that he might become the father of many nations, according to that which was spoken, So shall thy seed be. And being not weak in faith, he considered not his own body now dead, when he was about an hundred years old, neither yet the deadness of Sarah's womb: He staggered not at the promise of God through unbelief; but was strong in faith, giving glory to God; And being fully persuaded that, what he had promised, he was able also to perform. And therefore it was imputed to him for righteousness. (Romans 4:18–22)

> Through faith also Sara herself received strength to conceive seed, and was delivered of a child when she was past age, because she judged him faithful who had promised. (Hebrews 11:11)

3

Apostolic DNA

Without getting too deep into the science of genetics and bogging you down with a bunch of scientific jargon, let me give you a simple layman's overview.

DNA is a nucleic acid that contains the genetic instructions used in the development and functioning of all known living organisms. The main role of DNA molecules is the long-term storage of information. DNA is often compared to a set of blueprints, like a recipe or a code, since it contains the instructions needed to construct other components of cells such as proteins and RNA molecules.[12] Genes are distinct portions of a cell's DNA. Genes are packaged in bundles called chromosomes. Humans have twenty-three pairs of chromosomes with a total of forty-six. During conception, a child gets twenty-three chromosomes from its mother and twenty-three chromosomes from its father, with a total of forty-six.

Neil Cole points out that the DNA of the church consists of three distinct elements. The DNA is the pattern of kingdom life from the smallest unit (the disciple in relationship to Jesus and others) to the largest unit (a family or movement of churches). The pattern is the same, and its expression remains constant.

The key elements for healthy DNA

The DNA of the church can be simplified to three things, namely, divine truth, nurturing relationships, and apostolic mission. They are needed in every part of the church, from its smallest unit to its largest.

Divine truth. Truth comes from God. It is the revelation of God to humankind. This comes from the Son, the Spirit, and the scriptures. The Son (Jesus) is both God and human and came to reveal to us in his person what God is like and what God requires. The scriptures were authored by God and reveal God's unfolding plan for humanity. The Spirit of God is also divine truth, since he brings revelation and direction to believers.

Nurturing relationships. Humans were never created to be alone. We are social creatures and have an intrinsic need for relationships. Our relational orientation is a reflection of the image of God in us. God Himself is relational and exists in a community—Father, Son, and Holy Spirit. God is love because God is relational. To the Christian, God is love because he has always existed in relationship. Is love possible without someone to love? This should be the defining characteristic of our faith. All men should know that we are Christ's disciples by the love that we have for one another.

Apostolic mission. Apostolic means that someone is sent as a representative with a message. We are here for a purpose. We have been given a prime directive to fulfill—to make disciples of all the nations. This part of us also comes from the nature of God. Jesus is an apostle. He is the chief cornerstone of the apostolic foundation. Before he left this planet, he sent his disciples into the world with a mission[13].

As we have studied in detail how God made the first Adam in the book of Genesis, let's now consider the technology used by God to bring to birth the new creature—the last Adam.

Supernatural conception algorithm

> And the angel said unto her, Fear not, Mary: for thou hast found favour with God. And, behold, thou shalt conceive in thy womb, and bring forth a son, and shalt call his name JESUS. He shall be great, and shall be called the Son of the Highest: and the Lord God shall give unto him the throne of his father David: And he shall reign over the house of Jacob forever; and of his kingdom there shall be no end. Then said Mary unto the angel, How shall this be, seeing I know not a man? And the angel answered and said unto her, The Holy Ghost shall come upon thee, and the power of the Highest shall overshadow thee: therefore also that holy thing which shall be born of thee shall be called the Son of God. (Luke 1:30–35)

Prophecy is a creative technology of the Spirit. Whatever God speaks is prophetic (Isaiah 55:11). The prophetic word of God has the inherent power within itself to leave the invisible Spirit realm and manifest on the canvas of the physical world. Prior to this angel appearing to Mary, God began to prophesy in the book of Genesis about an apostolic seed, and he continued to prophesy through holy men about this seed (Isaiah 7:14) throughout the entire Old Testament. Now, after forty-two generations of framing and foreshadowing this seed with His word in clear intricate exact detail, God sends an angel to announce the arrival of the last Adam—his name, his rule, and his reign.

Rightfully, Mary asked the right question. How shall this be seeing I know not a man? This question is in line with what we have previously discussed—that is, that conception is the result of a male seed fertilizing a female seed. According to the angel, this last man Adam will be conceived in the womb of this young virgin woman. There can be no doubt, in order for this to happen, some type of supernatural transaction is about to take place. The scripture says that there are some things we can only understand through faith

(Hebrews11:3). So also, it is by faith we believe and accept the virgin birth of Christ. Additionally, because of Mary's question, the angel furnishes us with insight into the creative procedure and ingenuity of God. I call this the supernatural conception algorithm.

Holy Ghost + seed of the woman + overshadowing power of highest = supernatural conception = birth of the holy.

Let us look at this in more detail, then ask the question again and see if we can better illuminate the angel's answer to Mary. Holy Ghost or the word *pneuma*,[14] meaning the third person of the triune God, the Holy Spirit, coequal, coeternal with the Father and the Son. Seed or the word *zera*',[15] meaning the posterity of the woman (Genesis 3:15). Power or the word *dunamis*,[16] meaning strength, ability, inherent power residing by virtue of its nature that puts forth power for performing miracles. It is arising power consisting in or resting upon armies, forces, or host. Highest or the word *Hupsistos*,[17] meaning the most high of place or the highest regions of rank. Overshadow the word *Episkiazo*,[18] meaning a shining cloud surrounding and enveloping a person with brightness, the Holy Spirit exerting creative energy upon the womb of the Virgin Mary and impregnating it.

How shall this be seeing I know not a man?

The one who has the highest regions of rank (God) by His Holy Spirit will come upon you, Mary, with miracle power as a shining cloud surrounding and enveloping you with brightness; he will exert creative energy upon your womb and impregnate you.

Holiness: the DNA of deity

The angel also said a holy thing shall be born. This is a holy thing born of the Holy Spirit. It is a quickening life; it is life-giving "resurrection life." It is absolute perfection, absent of sin, uniquely and intimately associated with God's fundamental nature of holiness, the DNA of deity conceived in the womb of a woman. This is unequivocally the Son of God, the Word made flesh (John 1:14). The last Adam is born both human and deity; as Matt Slick points out, Jesus is one person with two natures.

Jesus is the most important person who has ever lived since he is Lord and Savior; God in human flesh. He is not half God and half man. He is fully divine and fully man. In other words, Jesus has two distinct natures: divine and human. Jesus is the Word who was God and was with God and was made flesh (John 1:1, 14). This means that in the single person of Jesus is both a human and divine nature; God and man.

The divine nature was not changed when the Word became flesh (John 1:1, 14). Instead, the Word was joined with humanity (Colossians 2:9). Jesus's divine nature was not altered. Also, Jesus is not merely a man who "had God within Him," nor is he a man who "manifested the God principle." He is God in flesh, second person of the Trinity. "The Son is the radiance of God's glory and the exact representation of his being, sustaining all things by his powerful word" (Hebrews 1:3). Jesus's two natures are not "mixed together" (Eutychianism), nor are they combined into a new God-man nature (Monophysitism). They are separate yet act as a unit in the one person of Jesus. This is called the Hypostatic union. The following chart should help you see the two natures of Jesus "in action":

GOD	MAN
He is worshiped (Matthew 2:2, 11; 14:33).	He worshiped the Father (John 17).
He was called God (John 20:28; Hebrews 1:8)	He is called man (Mark 15:39; John 19:5).
He was called Son of God (Mark 1:1)	He was called Son of Man (John 9:35-37)
He is prayed to (Acts 7:59).	He prayed to the Father (John 17).
He is sinless (1 Peter 2:22; Hebrews 4:15).	He was tempted (Matthew 4:1).
He knows all things (John 21:17).	He grew in wisdom (Luke 2:52).
He gives eternal life (John 10:28).	He died (Romans 5:8).

The communicatio idiomatum

A doctrine that is related to the Hypostatic union is the communicatio idiomatum (Latin for "communication of properties"). It is the teaching that the attributes of both the divine and human natures are ascribed to the one person of Jesus. This means that the man Jesus could lay claim to the glory he had with the Father before the world was made (John 17:5), claim that he descended from heaven (John 3:13), and also claim omnipresence (Matthew 28:20). All of these are divine qualities that are laid claim to by Jesus; therefore, the attributes of the divine properties were claimed by the person of Jesus.

One of the most common errors that non-Christian cults make is not understanding the two natures of Christ. For example, the Jehovah's Witnesses focus on Jesus's humanity and ignore his divinity. They repeatedly quote verses dealing with Jesus as a man and try and set them against scripture showing that Jesus is also divine. On the other hand, the Christian scientists do the reverse. They focus on the scriptures showing Jesus's divinity to the extent of denying his true humanity.

For a proper understanding of Jesus and, therefore, all other doctrines that relate to him, his two natures must be properly understood and defined. Jesus is one person with two natures. This is why he would grow in wisdom and stature (Luke 2:52) yet know all things (John 21:17). He is the divine Word that became flesh (John 1:1,14).

The Bible is about Jesus (John 5:39). The prophets prophesied about him (Acts 10:43). The Father bore witness of him (John 5:37; 8:18). The Holy Spirit bore witness of him (John 15:26). The works Jesus did bore witness of him (John 5:36; 10:25). The multitudes bore witness of him (John 12:17). And Jesus bore witness of himself (John 14:6; 18:6).

Other verses to consider when examining his Deity are John 10:30–33; 20:28; Colossians 2:9; Philippians 2:5–8; Hebrews 1:8–13; and 2 Peter 1:1. First Timothy 2:5 says, "For there is one God, and one mediator also between God and men, the man Christ Jesus." Right now, there is a man in heaven on the throne of God. He is our advocate with the Father (1 John 2:1). He is our Savior (Titus 2:13). He is our Lord (Romans 10:9–10). He is Jesus.[19]

Jesus is 100 percent man and 100 percent God. He is 100 percent human and 100 percent deity. The last man Adam which is the Lord is a life-giving spirit; he is the Christ, the anointed one, born of the Spirit. He is the last man Adam, a new creature never before seen.

Born from above

Jesus answered and said unto him, Verily, verily, I say unto thee, Except a man be born again, he cannot see the kingdom of God. Nicodemus saith unto him, How can a man be born when he is old? can he enter the second time into his mother's womb, and be born? Jesus answered, Verily, verily, I say unto thee, Except a man be born of water and of the Spirit, he cannot enter into the kingdom of God. That which is born of the flesh is flesh; and that which is born of the Spirit is spirit. (John 3:3–6)

A new creature; a new ethnos

> For in Christ Jesus neither circumcision availeth any thing, nor uncircumcision, but a new creature. (Galatians 6:15)

Creature means anything created, whether animate or inanimate; a person; a human being. The word *creature* is from the root word *create*, or to cause to come into being as something unique that would not naturally evolve or that is not made by ordinary processes.

The new creature represents an elimination of distinctions of all those that are in Christ. If you were White before you were born again, you are no longer that; if you were Black before you were born again, you are no longer that; if you were Jewish, Irish, Mexican, Muslim, in fact whatever you were before you were born again, you are no longer that; because distinctions are eliminated in Christ. We will take a closer look at this aspect of the doctrine of Christ in a later chapter. As we have seen, the last man Adam is born of God, making him both human and deity. Whereas the first man Adam was given creation or created life, the last man Adam was not born of life that was created but rather born from life that has always been. This is uncreated life, the life of God himself. This is life that gives life (1 Corinthians 15:45). This is endless, everlasting, perpetual, eternal, resurrection life. The last man Adam is a new firstfruits creature.

Firstfruits, translated from the Greek word *aparche*—a term used of persons consecrated to God for all time. Persons superior in excellence to others of the same class.[20]

> But now is Christ risen from the dead, and become the firstfruits of them that slept. For since by man came death, by man came also the resurrection of the dead. For as in Adam all die, even so in Christ shall all be made alive. But every man in his own order: Christ the firstfruits; afterward they that are Christ's at his coming. (1 Corinthians 15:20–23)

The last man Adam represents a firstfruits company, a new breed, a new class; he is the apostle and high priest of our confession; also, he is the apostle and high priest of a new ethnos.

Ethnos is an ethnic group. An ethnic group is a group of people whose members identify with each other through a common *heritage* often consisting of common language, a common culture often including a shared religion and an ideology that stresses common *ancestry* or *endogamy.*

The apostolic anointing

Over the last few years, there have been many well-written books teaching on the subject of the apostle that have helped us identify, recognize, and distinguish the operation of this gift by citing its function and works. Because of this, I will endeavor to be less exhaustive in this particular area but seek to impart a deeper and broader revelation and understanding of the word apostolic as it pertains to the body of Christ. Today, many fellowships use the word *apostolic* to describe core beliefs, denomination, or affiliation to convey vision. But what exactly is apostolic (other than of or pertaining to the apostles), and what does it mean to be apostolic? Before we proceed, let me give you this foundational statement. *Apostolic* extends beyond its function and works if you are born again; for you, apostolic is more than just a title; it is who you are.

> But as many as received him, to them gave he power to become the sons of God, even to them that believe on his name: Which were born, not of blood, nor of the will of the flesh, nor of the will of man, but of God. (John 1:12–13)

Everyone that has received Christ is a member of a holy ethnos (ethnic group). This ethnos is united by heritage, ancestry, and endogamy. Let us look at these.

Heritage is something someone is born into. The status, conditions, or character acquired by being born into a particular family or social class.

> For by one Spirit are we all baptized into one body, whether we be Jews or Gentiles, whether we be bond or free; and have been all made to drink into one Spirit. For the body is not one member, but many. (1 Corinthians 12:13–14)

> For ye are all the children of God by faith in Christ Jesus. For as many of you as have been baptized into Christ have put on Christ. There is neither Jew nor Greek, there is neither bond nor free, there is neither male nor female: for ye are all one in Christ Jesus. And if ye be Christ's, then

are ye Abraham's seed, and heirs according to the promise. (Galatians 3:26-29)

This all falls under the heading of "Spirit Baptism." The only way to become a part of the family of God (the body of Christ) is to be born into it. It will not happen just because you go to church, nor will it happen because you join a church. This is the baptism that makes you a new creature. The scripture says all believers are baptized into one body, and that body is Christ. This particular Spirit Baptism is rarely mentioned. The focus is most always on the results of this baptism, which is being born again. Later, we will unpack this truth to see its broader scope and how it impacts every believer. When an individual by faith accepts Jesus Christ as Lord and Savior, the Holy Spirit baptizes them into the body of Christ. They become heirs of God and joint-heirs with Christ, making them a part of the family of God. And because they are born of the Spirit (John 3:8) and of incorruptible seed (1 Peter 1:23), they take on God's divine nature and family heritage.

Ancestry refers to relatives who lived a long time ago. The people related to your family or ancestral descent.

Therefore it is of faith, that it might be by grace; to the end the promise might be sure to all the seed; not to that only which is of the law, but to that also which is of the faith of Abraham; who is the father of us all. (Romans 4:16)

Endogamy is marriage within a group or the social practice of marrying another member of the same clan, people, or other kinship group.

Be ye not unequally yoked together with unbelievers: for what fellowship hath righteousness with unrighteousness? And what communion hath light with darkness? (2 Corinthians 6:14)

All born-again believers are a part of this holy apostolic (ethnos) ethnic group.

> But ye are a chosen generation, a royal priest-
> hood, a holy nation, a peculiar people; that ye
> should shew forth the praises of him who hath
> called you out of darkness into his marvelous
> light; Which in time past were not a people,
> but are now the people of God: which had not
> obtained mercy, but now have obtained mercy.
> (1 Peter 2:9–10)

The apostle Peter says you are a chosen generation, a royal priesthood, a holy nation. The word ethnos[21] means a company, troop, and swarm; a multitude of individuals of the same nature or genus. Did you get that? Individuals *of the same nature*! The word genus means species. Everyone that is born again becomes a new species and a part of this holy ethnic group.

> Wherefore, holy brethren, partakers of the heav-
> enly calling, consider the Apostle and High Priest
> of our profession, Christ Jesus; (Hebrews 3:1)

As a sent one (an apostle), Jesus as firstfruits is the new pattern and prototype proton man. God made the first man Adam in his image and likeness. The last man Adam is the express image of God.

The last Adam is not made in the "tselem" image but rather the express image, the word "charakter" from the *Strong's Concordance charakter* (khar-ak-tare'), the exact expression (the image) of any person or thing, marked likeness, precise reproduction in every respect, i.e., facsimile, meaning the exact expression of any person or thing, marked likeness, precise reproduction in every respect.[22]

> Who being the brightness of his glory, and the
> express image of his person, and upholding all
> things by the word of his power, when he had by

> himself purged our sins, sat down on the right
> hand of the Majesty on high: Being made so
> much better than the angels, as he hath by inher-
> itance obtained a more excellent name than they.
> (Hebrews 1:3–4)

The last man Adam is the brightness of God's glory. This is Christ perfectly reflecting the majesty of God. He is Emmanuel, God with us. He is I AM, the name of deity.

> Then said the Jews unto him, Thou art not yet
> fifty years old, and hast thou seen Abraham?
> Jesus said unto them, Verily, verily, I say unto
> you, Before Abraham was, I am. (John 8:57–58)

The Technology of Spirit Baptism

Apart from the miracle birth and resurrection of Jesus Christ, the baptism of the Holy Spirit is a continuative demonstration of divine wisdom, understanding, and power displayed in the Bible and throughout history. This Spirit baptism separates the doctrine of Christ from all religions in the world.

> For as the body is one, and hath many members,
> and all the members of that one body, being
> many, are one body: so also is Christ. For by one
> Spirit are we all baptized into one body, whether
> we be Jews or Gentiles, whether we be bond or
> free; and have been all made to drink into one
> Spirit. (1 Corinthians 12:12–13)

This is one of the most important scriptures concerning the work of the Holy Spirit or the operation of the Holy Spirit as he identifies us with the body of Christ.

By definition, the baptism of the Holy Spirit found in 1 Corinthians 12:12–13 is the operation of the spirit of God as he, the Spirit relates to our relationship with God. The spirit of God has everything to do with our relationship with God. There is no relationship with God or the family of God outside of or apart from the Holy Spirit. Let's read verse 13 again, "For by one Spirit are we all baptized into one body, whether we be Jews or Gentiles, whether we be bond or free; and have been all made to drink into one Spirit."

This scripture plainly explains and gives the results of this Holy Spirit baptism. The spirit of God baptizes us into the one body. This one body according to verse 12 is the body of Christ. The only way a person gets into the body of Christ is by this Holy Spirit baptism, and let me point out that this has nothing to do with speaking in tongues or any of the other power gifts we will discuss in a latter segment. Now according to 1 Corinthians 12:12, there is only one body, but there are many members. For as the body is one, and hath many members, and all the members of that one body, being many, are one body: so also is Christ.

The topic here is the body of Christ. Notice how the scripture uses an allegory or metaphor of the physical, visible, natural human body to contrast the similarities of the spiritual, invisible, supernatural body of Christ. "For by one Spirit are we all baptized into one body, whether we be Jews or Gentiles, whether we be bond or free; and have been all made to drink into one Spirit" (verse 13). So we see that the one Spirit places us into the one body no matter who you are.

Also, according to scripture, this spirit baptism eliminates distensions. Distention is eliminated when anyone is baptized into the body of Christ. This means that whatever identity you had prior to this baptism, you no longer have that identification. In other words, whatever you or others labeled you as you are no longer that. Now this may sound radical, but we will find that it's exactly what the Bible teaches.

> For as many of you as have been baptized into
> Christ have put on Christ. There is neither Jew

> nor Greek, there is neither bond nor free, there
> is neither male nor female: for ye are all one in
> Christ Jesus. (Galatians 3:27–28)

Here we see the same phraseology witnessing to the fact that this spirit baptism removes distinctions between all-natural known classifications of people, Jew, Gentiles, Greek, bond, free…it even disavows the gender of male and female. This also includes the groupings by which we separate ourselves today African American, Anglo-Saxon, Mexican, Arab, and so forth. This spirit baptism is designed by God to eliminate and disavows all dissentions outside of Christ. I am persuaded to believe that it also pertains to every religious, traditional, and denominational distinction, and this truth is established by three separate New Testament scriptures: 1 Corinthians 12:13, Galatians 3:28, and Colossians 3:11.

These three scriptures establish and confirm God's will to disregard the divisions of all that are born into his kingdom. Because of this, we must also understand that in the mind of God, there is no such thing as a black or white Christian. According to scripture, there is no such thing as a Jewish or Gentile Christian, Catholic Christian, a Methodist Christian, Lutheran, Episcopalian, Pentecostal, or Baptist Christian or even a black church, a white church, Mexican church, Filipino church, and so on. These descriptive distinctions come from the fallen intellect of the old man and his way of thinking and doing things. But in the mind of God and according to Scripture, they simply do not exist in Christ.

As a result of this, we said earlier that whoever you were prior to this baptism, you are no longer that. So the question we should ask is, what or who does the Bible say we are after we've been baptized into the body of Christ?

> Therefore if any man be in Christ, he is a new
> creature: old things are passed away; behold, all
> things are become new. (2 Corinthians 5:17)

This scripture literally says that if any man is in Christ, he is *a new life-form* (hold that thought, I'll come back to it latter). This new creature or new life-form is the *one new man* found in Ephesians 2:15. In Colossians 3:10–11, it says, "And have put on the *new man*, which is renewed in knowledge after the image of him that created him: Where there is neither Greek nor Jew, circumcision nor uncircumcision, Barbarian, Scythian, bond nor free: but Christ is all, and in all. Being baptized into the body of Christ means you have been upgraded. You have been upgraded from the first Adam into the last Adam. Therefore, you have become a new creature." Let's look again at our foundational scripture, 1 Corinthians 12:12–13. This time from various translations.

In the Amplified Bible, it says, "For just as the body is a unity and yet has many parts, and all the parts, though many, form only one body, so it is with Christ (the Messiah, the Anointed One). For by means of the personal agency of one Holy Spirit, we were all, whether Jews or Greeks, slaves or free, baptized and by baptism united together into one body, and all made to drink of one Holy Spirit.

From the Good News Translation, Christ is like a single body, which has many parts. It is still one body, even though it is made up of different parts. In the same way, all of us, whether Jews or Gentiles, whether slaves or free, have been baptized into the one body by the same Spirit, and we have all been given the one spirit to drink.

Lastly, in the Message Bible, you can easily enough see how this kind of thing works by looking no further than your own body. Your body has many parts—limbs, organs, cells—but no matter how many parts you can name, you're still one body. It's exactly the same with Christ. By means of his one Spirit, we all said goodbye to our partial and piecemeal lives we each used to independently call our own shots, but then we entered into a large and integrated life in which he has the final say in everything. (This is what we proclaimed in word and action when we were baptized.) Each of us is now a part of his resurrection body, refreshed and sustained at one fountain—his Spirit—where we all come to drink. The old labels we once used to identify ourselves, labels like Jew or Greek, slave or free, are no longer useful. We need something larger, more comprehensive.

As we said before, this is one of the most important scriptures concerning the work and operation of the Holy Spirit as he identifying us with the body of Christ. The Amplified Bible makes it clear by saying that by means of the personal agency of one Holy Spirit, we were all baptized and, by baptism, united together into one body. The Message Bible states that anyone who takes part in this baptism become a part of Christ's resurrected body.

> For as many of you as were baptized into Christ into a spiritual union and communion with Christ, the Anointed One, the Messiah, have put on (clothed yourselves with) Christ. There is now no distinction neither Jew nor Greek, there is neither slave nor free, there is not male and female; for you are all one in Christ Jesus. (Galatians 3:27–28 Amplified Bible)

In this resurrected spiritual body, the designations that once described us no longer exist. Simply put, in Christ, there are no dissentions, there is *only* Christ. As all distinctions are abolished by this spirit baptism. That is not to say that while on this earth, we throw away the natural creation dynamics of man and woman intended for procreation. Yet scripture clearly reveals and establishes the intent and plan of God is to disavow all distinctions, including male and female gender of *all* who are baptized by the Holy Spirit into Christ. In fact, prior to the resurrection of Christ, in the mind of God, only two groupings of people existed. The Jews, God's chosen people and the gentiles, who had no promise, had no hope, and were without God in the world according to Ephesians 2:12.

Think about this for a moment, if you were a parent who named your child, then you of all people know who that child is. But if for some reason, that child did not respond to that name and went around calling his or herself something other than what you named them, you would be correct in concluding that your child is suffering from some sort a problem.

We said earlier that in the mind of God, distinctions in Christ do not exist. However, when we look at the body of Christ today, all we see are distinctions. Therefore, just as you would as a parent, it's logical for us to conclude also that the church (Ecclesia) lacks revelation concerning who she really is. Scripture dictates that it is the will and design of God to eliminate all distinctions of all that are born into his kingdom by creating one new man in Christ. Now let's take a deeper dive so we can see precisely what the scriptures reveal. This may be a bit shocking, but I challenge you to search the scriptures as did the Bereans and see whether these things are so (Acts 17:11).

"Therefore, if any person is ingrafted in Christ [the Messiah] he is a new creation [a new creature altogether]; the old [previous moral and spiritual condition] has passed away. Behold, the fresh and new has come!" (2 Corinthians 5:17 Amplified Bible). It says if any person is ingrafted in Christ, he is a new creature altogether.

(In this new creation, all distinctions vanish.) "There is no room for and there can be neither Greek nor Jew, circumcised nor uncircumcised, nor difference between nations whether alien barbarians or Scythians who are the most savage of all, nor slave or free man; but Christ is all and in all everything and everywhere, to all men, without distinction of person" (Colossians 3:11 Amplified Bible). Let me add that is does not get any clearer than this.

Since we know that it is the will of God to remove all distinctions in Christ and according to scripture, if we are no longer who we were prior to this spirit baptism, again the question is, what or who does the Bible say we are after we have been baptized into Christ?

If any man be in Christ, he is a *new creature*. The word *creature* defined in the Strong's Concordance is a thing created or individual things, beings or anything created. A dictionary definition of the word *creature* is an animal, especially a nonhuman, the creatures of the woods and fields. But look at this definition, a creature from outer space (www.dictionary.com). Now some of you reading or listening to this may think that what I am about to say is blasphemy. The dictionary said a creature is from outer space, but how about a creature or being from heaven? Now please put your stones down and follow me for a moment. This may seem farfetched, but contrary to what you may have seen on *Star Trek*, we have far more biblical evidence to prove this fact than we do in proving that alien life exists on other planets or in some faraway galaxy.

> Anyone who is joined to Christ is a new being;
> the old is gone, the new has come. (2 Corinthians
> 5:17 Good News Bible)

A new being literally means a new life-form. In the book of Ephesians, it not only tells us about the creation of this new life-form but also tells us how this life-form is created and the author of its creation.

"For by grace are ye saved through faith; and that not of yourselves: it is the gift of God: Not of works, lest any man should boast. For we are his workmanship, created in Christ Jesus unto good works, which God hath before ordained that we should walk in them" (Ephesians 2:8–10). This scripture tells us that the born-again experience that saved us from eternal damnation is a gift from God, and it says that we are God's workmanship created in Christ Jesus. What then is this workmanship?

> Having abolished in his flesh the enmity, even the
> law of commandments contained in ordinances;
> for to make in himself of twain one new man so
> making peace. (Ephesians 2:15)

This is the work Christ did on the cross at Calvary. The word *twain* means two these are the two grouping of people mentioned earlier (Jew and Gentiles). The new creature, new being, or new life-form is the one new man found here in Ephesians 2:15. This one new man is the workmanship or creation of God, and according to scripture, this one new man was not made like the man that God made in Genesis 2:7, who received the breath of life into his nostrils and became a living soul or breathing creature. This one new man is the *new creature*, which is the product of God's workmanship that he created in Christ Jesus. This *one new man* was not made a living soul or natural breathing creature. God made this one new man a life-giving spirit.

> And so it is written, the first man Adam was made a living soul; the last Adam was made a quickening spirit. Howbeit that was not first which is spiritual, but that which is natural; and afterward that which is spiritual. The first man is of the earth, earthy; the second man is the Lord from heaven. (1 Corinthians 15:45–47)

Did you catch that? It says *the second man is the Lord from heaven.* According to this scripture, if we want to find a new life-form, we don't need to go to outer space, we don't need to look to the stars, we know it's not on the moon, and it's certainly not on Mars. The new life-form is *here* because the new creature came to this planet born of God two thousand years ago (Luke 1:35).

I know that all of this may seem like a scene from a science fiction movie, but the question you should ask is, can this be proven, is there evidence of a new class of human beings on earth, do they actually exist, and can we prove it biblically?

Scripture records the first citing of this new class of human beings, in the book of Acts 11:26. And when he had found him, he brought him unto Antioch. And it came to pass, that a whole year, they assembled themselves with the church and taught much people. And the disciples were called Christians first in Antioch. Again, the one new man is a Christ Class man and Jesus the last Adam was the prototype of this new Christ Class, humanity. Also, see Acts 4:13.

The baptism of the Holy Ghost found in 1 Corinthians 12:13 is the technology of the spirit of God, whereby his workmanship, he creates in Christ Jesus the new creature, new being, or new life-form, which is the one new man found in Ephesians 2:15. It is by this spirit baptism that we are all baptized by one spirit, into the one body of this one new man who is Messiah. We are all baptized by one Spirit, into the one body of the anointed one.

One New Man

God is a God of purpose, and we have seen through the scriptures that by God's own will and handiwork has removed all distinctions, even disavowing male and female in Christ. Now let's examine in detail why he chose to do so.

> Having abolished in the flesh the enmity, *even* the law of commandments *contained* in ordinances; that he might create in himself of the two one new man, *so* making peace; and might reconcile them both in one body unto God through the cross, having slain the enmity thereby. (Ephesians 2:15–16 American Standard)

> He brought an end to the commandments and demands found in Moses's teachings so that he could take Jewish and non-Jewish people and create one new humanity in himself. So he made peace. He also brought them back to God in one body by his cross, on which he killed the hostility. (Ephesians 2:15–16 (God's Word Translation)

> The Messiah has made things up between us so that we're now together on this, both non-Jewish outsiders and Jewish insiders. He tore down the wall we used to keep each other at a distance. He repealed the law code that had become so clogged with fine print and footnotes that it hindered more than it helped. Then he started over. Instead of continuing with two groups of people separated by centuries of animosity and

suspicion, he created a new kind of human being,
a fresh start for everybody. (Ephesians 2:15–16
Message Bible Translation)

These translations give us crystal clear insight into what the Bible refers to as the workmanship of God. The American Standard Bible calls this workmanship, one new quality of humanity. God's Word Translation says, "He created a new humanity in himself." The Message Bible states, "He created a new kind of human being." The descriptions used here to describe the product of God's workmanship in Christ are astonishing and almost unbelievable. Today, if you asked a scientist to define this verse of scripture in scientific terms from a pure scientific perspective, he or she would tell you that God has created a new human species. This is not science fiction; it's right here in the Bible.

The scripture states if any man be in Christ, he is a new creature, and according to our study, if you are a new creature, you are a new being or new life-form. This is the born-again experience, and it takes place when a person is baptized by the one spirit into one body which is the body of Christ. As a result of this spirit baptism, you become a part of a new human species, a holy ethnos (see 1 Peter 2:9 and Revelation 5:9–10). This is the workmanship of God.

First John 5:1 says, "Whosoever believeth that Jesus is the Christ is born of God." If you are born of God, you have the traits or the DNA of God's divine nature in you. "But he that is joined unto the Lord is one spirit" (1 Corinthians 6:17). Spiritually, you are one with God, your spirit has been mingled with his Spirit, you have been born of God, and God is your Father (Romans 8:15).

This new divine nature is the personality or character of God. This new divine nature is what makes you a new creature. This new nature is found in the one new man that you have been baptized into. Again, this is the born-again experience. By his workmanship, God has created in Christ a new class or classification of human beings or a new human species. Astonishing, isn't it? The one new man is a Christ Class man, and Jesus as the last Adam is the prototype of a new Christ Class, humanity. Now let's shift our focus a bit and look at the intent and purpose of this new human species from God's perspective.

> For as by one man's disobedience many were made sinners, so by the obedience of one shall many be made righteous. (Romans 5:19)

Before the foundation of the world, God purposed that in Jesus Christ, humanity would be redeemed and brought back to his glorious likeness.

> For whom he foreknew, he also predestined to be conformed to the image of his Son, that he might be the firstborn among many brethren. (Romans 8:29)

In this doctrine of Christ (Hebrews 6:1–2), God's divine wisdom and supernatural power is unrivaled, unavailable, and absent in all the religions of the world. Br. Oduro Collins in his book, *How Many Ways to Heaven*, says,

> Why is it that in some countries like Saudi Arabia, bible distribution is banned? Is it because the leaders of these countries fear the well-established claim by Christians that the Word have power to change, transform or convert souls? If it is true that the authorities in these countries worship the true God and Christians worship a pseudo-God as some claim then why should they fear the Bible and other Christian literature? Why don't they allow the distribution of the Bible without fear or persecution as the Christians do to other religious materials and books in predominantly Christian countries? (Collins Oduro, *How Many Ways to Heaven: God of No Contradiction. Arise*

to True Christianity. Revival Waves of Glory, p. 4
Kindle Edition)

The baptism of the Holy Spirit in 1 Corinthians 12:13 is the born-again experience. It is the spiritual technology whereby God's own handiwork brings salvation and restores his image and character to his fallen creation by creating one new man in Christ who is the exact expression of himself. But that's not all, through Christ, man is restored to his original purpose and design of blessedness, fruitfulness, and dominion over all the earth.

So who does the Bible say you are after you have been baptized into Christ?

> But as many as received him, to them gave he power to become the sons of God, even to them that believe on his name: Which were born, not of blood, nor of the will of the flesh, nor of the will of man, but of God. (John 1:12–13)

The Technology of Speaking in Unknown Tongues

While there have been many comprehensive books written on the subject of speaking in tongues, in this section, we will be less exhaustive and look rather to some of the less visited insights and newly discovered scientific facts concerning this subject.

Perhaps, one of the most controversial topics among biblical scholars and many within the body of Christ today is the gift of speaking in tongues and/or speaking in unknown tongues. For many years, this spiritual gift found in 1 Corinthians 12 has been shunned and, in some cases, downright rejected in several denominations. Some Christians have been instructed to stay away from it altogether because it is of the devil, or they have been taught that the gift passed away with the apostles misrepresenting 1 Corinthians 13:8 to prove their religious predisposition. Still others have been taught that this gift is not for every believer misconstruing 1 Corinthians 12:29–30, where tongues and interpretation of tongues is listed as a ministry gift that God has set in the church. Just as the other spiritual gifts of prophecy and knowledge mentioned in 1 Corinthians 13:8 have not passed away the gift of tongues and unknown tongues is also still active in the body of Christ today and will continue until the return of Jesus.

Let me say one more thing before we move on. One of the most and arguably the most powerful demonic force that Jesus contended with when he walked the earth was the spirit of religion, and religion is a spirit that we still contend with today. The spirit of religion can be so strong in some people that they will not allow the Bible to interfere with what they believe, yet the only deliverance from religion is biblical truth.

It is interesting to note that all the gifts of the Spirit—the word of wisdom, the word of knowledge, gift of faith, gifts of healings, working of miracles, prophecy, and discerning of spirits were all operational in the Old Testament economy; but these two of three vocal gifts or gifts of utterance—tongues and interpretation of tongues are absent and are only indicative to the New Testament experience. Yet when we look at Acts 2:3, we see that the supernatural gift of speaking in unknown tongues was used by God to set ablaze the birthing of the New Testament church.

On that day, the apostle Peter ties the manifestation of the gifts in the Old Testament and New Testaments economy's together with three words, Peter said this is that.

But this is that which was spoken by the prophet Joel, "And it shall come to pass in the last days, saith God, I will pour out of my Spirit upon all flesh: and your sons and your daughters shall prophesy, and your young men shall see visions, and your old men shall dream dreams: and on my servants and on my handmaidens I will pour out in those days of my Spirit; and they shall prophesy" (Acts 2:16–18).

Peter quotes the Old Testament passage where the prophet Joel prophesies, saying, "And it shall come to pass afterward, that I will pour out my spirit upon all flesh; and your sons and your daughters shall prophesy, your old men shall dream dreams, your young men shall see visions" (Joel 2:28).

Note, the prophet Joel says that the result of God pouring out his Spirit on all flesh will be prophesy, dreams, and visions. There is no mention of tongues. How can this be? How can Peter say that this speaking in tongues is that prophesy, dreams, and visions?

The Scripture is replete of different aspects and diversity of the operation of tongues. Keep in mind that the ministry gift of speaking in tongues found in 1 Corinthians 12 requires the gift of interpretation of tongues. Let's look at the three characteristics of tongues that will encompass this study. Number one, on the day of Pentecost, tongues became a sign to unbelievers. Number two, throughout Scripture, we see that the baptism in the Holy Spirit is in most but not all cases are evidenced by speaking in tongues. Lastly, remember Peter said *this is that* meaning, that speaking in tongues is equal to prophecy, vision and dreams. How does Peter come to this conclusion? Here is what Jesus said just before his ascension, "But ye shall receive power, after that the Holy Ghost is come upon you: and ye shall be witnesses unto me both in Jerusalem, and in all Judaea, and in Samaria, and unto the uttermost part of the earth" (Acts 1:8).

In this verse, Jesus prophesies to his disciples about the baptism in the Holy Spirit (Mathew 3:11, Mark 1:8, Luke 3:16), and he explains how they and we are to designate this experience. It is an explosive experience with power the Greek word *dunamis* from which we get the English word *dynamite*. The Bible uses various phrases to describe this supernatural experience such as "filled with the Holy Ghost" (Acts 2:4), "fell on them" (Acts 10:44–46), "endued with power from on high" (Luke 24:49), "Holy Ghost is come upon you" (Acts 1:8), "Holy Ghost came on them" (Acts 19:6), "poured out" (Acts 10:45), and "anointed" (Acts 10:38).

Notice when Jesus refers to the baptism in the Holy Spirit, he does not say you shall receive speaking in tongues, nor does he say you will receive prophecy, visions, or dreams. Yet Peter says this is that. What Peter is saying is that speaking in tongues is equivalent to prophecy, visions, and dreams. It is the supernatural power to witness and proclaim the gospel of the kingdom.

Now let's take a moment and look at what the Bible reveals about the different aspects of speaking in tongues or an unknown tongue. First, we need to understand that a tongue is a language. If you are reading or listening to this book, your native tongue could be English, yet there are also other languages that you know about but do not speak.

When the Bible refers to speaking in an unknown tongue, it does not mean that the tongue or language is unknown to everyone, but that it is unknown to the person speaking it. Meaning that the person who is speaking is supernaturally speaking a language that they have never learned. This is supernatural power. Today we have testimonies of evangelist who have gone into remote villages and having no translator nor previous understanding of the dialect were able to supernaturally speak the native language and lead people to Christ. We see this phenomenon in the second chapter of the book of Acts.

And they were all amazed and marveled, saying one to another, "Behold, are not all these which speak Galileans? And how hear we every man in our own tongue, wherein we were born?" (Acts 2:7–8).

The above scripture shows the spirit of God initiating tongues or in this case unknown tongues as a sign to unbelievers. Next, because there are different administrations and diversities of the operation of tongues, we must contrast this verse with 1 Corinthians 14:2.

> For he that speaketh in an unknown tongue speaketh not unto men, but unto God: for no man understandeth him; howbeit in the spirit he speaketh mysteries. (1 Corinthians 14:2 NJV)

On the surface, this seems contradictive to the prior verse. However, this scripture reveals still another dimension of tongues that some refers to as a devotional or personal prayer language. According to the apostle Paul's doctrine, a person who is baptized in the Spirit has an option of praying and singing according to their natural understanding or praying and singing from their spirit without understanding.

> For if I pray in an unknown tongue, my spirit prayeth, but my understanding is unfruitful. What is it then? I will pray with the spirit, and I will pray with the understanding also: I will sing with the spirit, and I will sing with the understanding also. (1 Corinthians 14:14–15)

While it is common for us to pray in the understanding of our natural language, you may ask why would anyone pray without understanding how is that in any way beneficial? I am glad you asked.

First of all, according to the apostle Paul's revelation, when we pray in an unknown tongue, we are not speaking to men we are speaking mysteries to God. It is a mystery because no one including ourselves know what we are saying. Next, he says when we pray in an unknown tongue our understanding is unfruitful. He is literally saying that our mind or intellectual faculty is unproductive in the process of praying (we will see scientific proof of this).

This is very important because there are times when we know that we need to pray, but we do not know what to pray or how we should pray. Also, we must remember that we are at war with the enemy of our soul. While the enemy does know a lot about us, he is not omniscient. In a natural battle, armed forces can deploy different operational tactics against an opposing army, one of which is called radio silence. It is used to hide the positioning of troops before a forthcoming attack. Another tactic deployed by the military is a communications code where coded messages are sent, but the communications are not understood by the enemy because the message is encoded. A good illustration of this is seen in the movie, *Windtalkers*, where two US Marines in World War II are assigned to protect Navajo Marines, who use their native language as an unbreakable radio cipher.

God Comms. Speaking in an unknown tongue is what I call God Comms, divine supernatural communication. The word *comms* is the short form of communications. It is used to refer to methods of sending messages, especially long-distance methods such as radio, telephone, Internet, and to the messages themselves. https://dictio-nary.cambridge.org/us/dictionary/english/comms

So what does all of this mean? It means that when we pray in tongues or an unknown tongue, we are praying over a spiritually encrypted network linked directly to God that no one can hack and no one can decipher. This encrypted network is hosted by the Holy Spirit. Speaking in tongues is a spiritual mode of communications that the enemy cannot decipher, cannot infiltrate, and therefore, a weapon that he cannot overthrow or defeat (2 Corinthians 10:3–4).

> Likewise the Spirit also helpeth our infirmities: for we know not what we should pray for as we ought: but the Spirit itself maketh intercession for us with groanings which cannot be uttered. And he that searcheth the hearts knoweth what is the mind of the Spirit, because he maketh intercession for the saints according to the will of God. (Romans 8:26–27 KJV)

> In the same way, the Spirit helps us in our weakness. We do not know what we ought to pray for, but the Spirit himself intercedes for us with groans that words cannot express. And he who searches our hearts knows the mind of the Spirit, because the Spirit intercedes for the saints in accordance with God's will. (Romans 8:26–27 NIV)

> And the Holy Spirit helps us in our distress. For we don't even know what we should pray for, nor how we should pray. But the Holy Spirit prays for us with groanings that cannot be expressed in words. And the Father who knows all hearts knows what the Spirit is saying, for the Spirit pleads for us believers in harmony with God's own will. (Romans 8:26 –27 NLT)

Centuries ago, in his epistle to the Corinthians (1 Corinthians 14:14), the apostle Paul wrote, "For if I pray in an unknown tongue, my spirit prayeth but my understanding is unfruitful." The scripture says, "God is a Spirit: and they that worship him must worship him in spirit and in truth" (John 4:24). In Jude 1:20, it says, "But ye, beloved, building up yourselves on your most holy faith, praying in the Holy Ghost." But that's not all, in Ephesians 6:18, praying in the Spirit is enumerated in the lineup of the whole armor of God as an offense weapon against the enemy.

This is our encrypted network linked directly to God where we not only worship our Father in spirit and truth, but we are also energized or built up as we speak to him in intimate unhindered sanctity. This means that when born-again believers pray in an unknown tongue, their spirit is communicating directly with God outside of their intellect. Science confirms scripture. Today, scientist have proven that God Comm's, direct divine supernatural communications with God exists.

A University Study Supports Bible Explanation of Speaking in Tongues

The neuroscience department in the medical school at the University of Pennsylvania conducted a provocative study on speaking in tongues and the effects it has on the brain. The doctor overseeing the study was Dr. Andrew Newberg, associate professor in the department of radiology and psychiatry and adjunct professor in the department of religious studies. He is also board certified in internal medicine, nuclear medicine, and nuclear cardiology. Dr. Newberg said, regarding those subjects who were studied while speaking in tongues, "We noticed a number of changes that occurred functionally in the brain. Our finding of decreased activity in the frontal lobes during the practice of speaking in tongues is fascinating because these subjects truly believed that the Spirit of God is moving through them and controlling what was being spoken."[2] For those who don't know, the frontal lobe helps us achieve our day-to-day activities such as thinking, reasoning, planning, managing and controlling emotions. In addition, it aids in making decisions, solving problems and even speaking. Newberg's research revealed that when the participants in his study sang gospel songs in English, the frontal lobes were alert and active, showing the subjects had to think about what they were saying or singing. However, when they sang and spoke in tongues the activity in the frontal lobe was nearly non-existent. Dr. Newberg also conducted the same test on a local pastor, finding that "the scan showed that the frontal lobe, the part of the brain that controls language, was active when he prayed in English. But for the most part fell quiet when he prayed in tongues."[3] It is a fact that the frontal-lobe activity increases when a person focuses on what they are saying. This finding confirms that when people speak in tongues, the words coming forth originate from a source other than the mind. In addition, it was revealed that while blood flow to the frontal lobes decreased, activity in the area that controls self-awareness was active.

This is interesting. This reveals that the subjects knew what was happening around them, and that they were not out of control or in some kind of mystical trance.

Dr. Newberg says, "Our brain imaging research shows us that these subjects are not in control of the usual language centers during this activity (when praying in tongues)." He further stated to ABC News, "It's not language, it's not regular language, at least that would normally activate the frontal lobe [of the brain]."[4] He adds, "These findings could be interpreted as the subjects' sense of self being taken over by something else. We scientifically assume it's being taken over by another part of the brain, but we couldn't see where it took place."

What does all this mean, and what does it substantiate? First, often it seems that science and the Bible are in conflict with one another. This study goes a long way in affirming the value of praying in tongues. Second, the study revealed that the frontal lobe of the brain is highly active when we speak and pray in our native language, but the activity of the frontal lobe decreases significantly when we pray in tongues. Thus, certifying what Paul said, "When I pray in tongues my spirit prays, but my understanding is unfruitful" (1

Corinthians 14:14). The apostle Paul knew two thousand years ago what this study only recently validated. Praying in tongues comes from your spirit, not your brain (*Speaking in Tongues: Your Secret Weapon* by Todd Smith, p. 21. Kindle Edition).

Praying and Singing in Tongues Boots Immune System

Carl Peterson, MD, a brain specialist, conducted a study on the relationship between the brain and speaking in tongues. In part, his study highlighted the physical benefits of praying in tongues. He worked on this study at ORU in Tulsa, Oklahoma. There are many intriguing facts that surfaced during his study; one of which was when we spend extended times in prayer and/or worship in the Spirit (using our heavenly prayer language), there is an activity that begins to take place in our brain. As we pray in tongues, the brain begins to release two chemical secretions that are directed into our immune systems, giving a 34 to 40 percent boost to the immune system. According to Dr. Peterson, "A very significant percentage of the central nervous system is directly and indirectly activated in the process of extended verbal and musical prayer (tongues and singing in tongues) over a period of time. This results in a significant release of brain hormones which, in turn, increases the body's general immunity" (Todd Smith, *Speaking in Tongues: Your Secret Weapon*, pp. 6–7. Kindle Edition).

4

Apostolic Reformation

Reformation is recurrent. God deploys apostles to bring reform. Apostolic reformation is nothing new. It is visible throughout the history of the Lord's dealing with his kingdom, and *ekklesia*, commonly referred to today as the church. From the reformation of Judaism to first-century Christianity, the movement in the sixteenth century that led to the reform of Catholicism and the establishment of the Protestant faith, and the most recent reformation of the baptism of the Holy Spirit at Azusa Street in the early nineteen hundreds, reformation is recurrent.

The root word of reformation is the word reform which simply means to correct or to form again, to put or change into an improved form or condition, to amend or improve by change of form or removal of faults or abuses, to put an end to (an evil) by enforcing or introducing a better method or course of action, and to induce or cause to abandon evil ways.[23] The 1828 Webster definitions of reform are to change from worse to better, to amend, to correct, to restore to a former good state, or to bring from a bad to a good state; as to reform a profligate man; to reform corrupt manners or morals.[24] Reformation brings revival, which has always been God's mechanism to counteract spiritual decline. Reformation facilitates change and transformation, making spiritual upgrade possible in the church. Whenever the church falls beneath her privilege or birthright, reformation revives her and brings back the light, purity, and power that exemplified the first-century *ekklesia*. History shows that spiritual upgrade is revelatory, and is established by the reformation of current revelation knowledge of recovered spiritual truth.

The apostle, like the prophet, is a bearer of divine revelation. Since this revelation is fulfilled in Christ, a new term is needed in place of the "prophet," a term which corresponds to the new situation but still refers to the divine commission. The NT prophets, of course, do not correspond to those of the OT, though they are held in high regard. It is the apostle who has in the new situation the function of the prophet in the old.[25]

When polluted religious systems take the church off course, and the view of God's kingdom becomes obscure, blurred, and out of focus, God raises up apostles to put the church back on track and realign its focal point by clearly demonstrating the power of the kingdom. Jesus was a reformer. He came preaching the kingdom of God and demonstrated the kingdom by healing the sick, casting out devils, and raising the dead. The Apostle Paul was also a reformer. Paul, after being radically reformed himself from Judaism and born into the body of Christ, did not depend on his training from Gamaliel, a doctor of the law (Acts 22:3), nor did he preach from philosophies employing natural wisdom; but like Jesus, he demonstrated the technologies of the Spirit.

> And my speech and my preaching was not with enticing words of man's wisdom, but in demonstration of the Spirit and of power: That your faith should not stand in the wisdom of men, but in the power of God. (1 Corinthians 2:4–5)

The Spirit is indispensable, for in the Spirit (Pentecost), the apostles receive assurance of Christ's presence and power and a standard of what is to be done as the apostles dedicate themselves to God's will and aim at faith in the hearers rather than personal achievement as preachers or healers. The accompanying works are displays of Christ's power, which validate the divine message as fact and not just theory. They are indispensable not to the messengers but to the message. The thinking relating to these apostolic signs finds its model in Moses as the divine messenger endorsed by signs (Exodus 3:12).[26] The technologies (miracles, signs, and wonders) and power of the Spirit demonstrate the authenticity of the Gospel of Christ, causing people to repent of their dead works and rightly focus their faith toward God to receive forgiveness of sin.

The apostle Paul spent two years teaching the gospel in Ephesus at the school of Tyrannus. The scripture says that after these two years, all of Asia, both Jews and Greeks, heard the word of the Lord Jesus. In Ephesus, God authored special technologies of the Spirit (Acts 19:9–11). The apostle Paul used this revelatory insight to develop an apostolic strategy to reach the sick with healing and to cast out devils from those that were demon-possessed. Because of this demonstration of the Spirit and power, the influence of darkness was broken over groups of individuals that practiced the occult, including a Jewish chief priest and his seven sons who were exorcists. Assuming that the gospel of Christ was just another type of magic or conjuring, they tried their method of exorcism using the name of Jesus, perhaps as an incantation on a fierce demoniac, and miserably failed (Acts 19:14–16). This caused many of the exorcists and those who secretly practiced the occult to repent publicly and destroy their occult paraphernalia. This extreme reformation sparked revival. As the people of Ephesus (feared) reverenced the Lord, the name of Jesus was exalted.

> Many of them also which used curious arts
> brought their books together, and burned them
> before all men: and they counted the price of
> them, and found it fifty thousand pieces of silver.
> So mightily grew the word of God and prevailed.
> (Acts 19:19–20)

The power of God is not capricious, for it expresses his will and is thus determined by his righteousness (Isaiah 5:16). Having the inner energy of holiness, it is effective as the power of judgment and grace, and it serves the manifestation and magnification of his glory

(Psalm 24:8). All ideas of magic are thus excluded. We are brought into the sphere of a relationship in which obedience, prayer, and sacrifice replace incantations and rituals. The uniqueness of the Old Testament concept of God and his power issues in doxologies which have parallels in other religions but which are distinguished by their reference to the mighty acts of God in history and by the glow of joy in God, of passion, and of experience of God.[27]

Religion, witchcraft, and the traditions of men are just a few of the beguiling spirit powers of Satan that keep people in bondage. Apostles and those that flow in this apostolic prophetic dimension (this will be discussed more in the next section) have the ability, by the power of the Spirit, to break these influences and turn people, cities, and even nations from the power of Satan to God (Acts 26:18).

It was by the demonstration of the Spirit and of power that Elijah (an apostolic OT type) turned the nation of Israel from Baal worship back to God by calling down fire from on high and bringing revival to the land (1 Kings 18:37–39). The people in Samaria bewitched by sorcery were delivered and set free from witchcraft when they saw and heard the miracles that Philip did. Although Philip was not an apostle, nor did the apostles at Jerusalem send him, he was a part of this apostolic team. Philip, in the midst of persecution, led by the Holy Spirit, went to Samaria and preached Christ to them. As a result, many were saved, healed, and delivered. Here, also we witness the functioning of Apostolic Team Ministry (ATM) by impartation of Peter and John for the people to receive the baptism of the Holy Ghost (Acts 8:14–17).

> God raises up apostles to put the church back on track and realign its focal point by clearly demonstrating the power of kingdom.

> Then Philip went down to the city of Samaria, and preached Christ unto them. And the people with one accord gave heed unto those things which Philip spake, hearing and seeing the miracles which he did. For unclean spirits, crying with

> loud voice, came out of many that were possessed
> with them: and many taken with palsies, and that
> were lame, were healed. And there was great joy
> in that city. (Acts 8:5–8)

Because of God's favor, the nation of Israel became the reservoir of divine spiritual truth, and all spiritual technology was first given to Israel. They were entrusted with the kingdom of God. This kingdom was unlike other empires and governments. This kingdom was different in that it was not ruled by man. It was a theocracy ruled and governed by Almighty God himself. The Lord God was Israel's king. They were the most blessed nation on the face of the earth, and no other nation could stand before them as they walked in obedience to God's word. However, corruption crept into the temple hierarchy. Judaism (the old wineskin) split into three major factions: the wealthy Sadducees, the fanatically religious Zealots, and the mainstream majority Pharisees, and the scribes who were not a sect but teachers of the Law. Judaism came under the sway of evil, and its leadership (bound by religious demons) began to abuse the authority that God had given them. By the time Jesus came, this blessed nation had become the most wicked and demonized generation of its time (Matthew 12:44). Jesus called them a generation of vipers (poisonous snakes). It was a generation full of religious demons, a generation of leaders full of hypocrisy, and a generation that would not repent (Matthew 12:41–45). Jesus rebuked them sharply and accused the experts of the law (scribes) of not fulfilling their commission of teaching the people. They were supposed to enlighten the people by expounding the law; instead, they kept the people in darkness. He called them hypocrites and accused them of shutting up the kingdom of heaven.

> Woe unto you, lawyers! for ye have taken away
> the key of knowledge: ye entered not in your-
> selves, and them that were entering in ye hin-
> dered. (Luke11:52)

> But woe unto you, scribes and Pharisees, hyp-
> ocrites! For ye shut up the kingdom of heaven
> against men: for ye neither go in yourselves, nei-
> ther suffer ye them that are entering to go in.
> (Matthew 23:13)

Religious spirits have a goal and an objective. The main goal of religious spirits is to influence leadership in church government, and its main objective is to kill the prophets. The prophets are important in the local church. Prophets can recognize apostolic authority. They are many times used by God to identify and activate true apostolic leadership. John the Baptist, before baptizing him, identified (the apostolic seed in Genesis 3:15) Jesus as the Lamb of God, and Elijah anointed Jehu king over Israel in the Old Testament.

When Jesus came demonstrating the kingdom, these demonized leaders had gotten so far off course that they did not even recognize him as Messiah. They cut deals with the Roman government to put him to death because they did not want to lose their position of authority as rulers over of the kingdom and nation of Israel.

> Then gathered the chief priests and the Pharisees
> a council, and said, What do we? For this man
> doeth many miracles. If we let him thus alone, all
> men will believe on him: and the Romans shall
> come and take away both our place and nation.
> (John 11:47–48)

The Jewish leaders had become so twisted in their thinking; they exaggerated the importance of customs and the traditions of men, thereby making the word of God ineffective, leaving a nation of God's chosen people sick and oppressed. The leaders lorded over the people rather than healing and releasing those who were oppressed by the devil. They left them bound, offering little or no aid for their afflictions, when it was God's will that they be free, healed, and delivered. Jesus came to deliver the lost sheep of Israel and to salvage the kingdom of God that was being abused and had become contaminated by religious devils. He took the kingdom from religious leadership and the nation of Israel and gave the kingdom to the *ekklesia* (Matthew 16:19).

> Therefore say I unto you, The kingdom of God shall be taken from you, and given to a nation bringing forth the fruits thereof. (Matthew 21:43)

Leaders in the synagogue became heartless, void of compassion for the people, and because of this corruption in the temple hierarchy, those that had covenant rights to healing and deliverance were left in bondage because rules and regulations had taken precedence over the Word of God.

> The Lord then answered him, and said, Thou hypocrite, doth not each one of you on the sabbath lose his ox or his ass from the stall, and lead him away to watering? And ought not this woman, being a daughter of Abraham, whom Satan hath bound, lo, these eighteen years, be loosed from this bond on the sabbath day? (Luke 13:15–16)

God used the rod of the Romans to bring judgment on this wicked generation just as Jesus prophesied.

> For the days shall come upon thee, that thine enemies shall cast a trench about thee, and compass thee round, and keep thee in on every side, And shall lay thee even with the ground, and thy children within thee; and they shall not leave in thee one stone upon another; because thou knewest not the time of thy visitation. (Luke 19:43–44)

This judgment was against a generation that would not repent. This generation missed their time of visitation. God sent them prophets and wise men to warn them that they were in violation of covenant, but they refused to listen. They murdered the messengers of the Lord, and as a result came under judgment for all the righteous bloodshed from Abel to Zacharias. This was fulfilled in AD 70, when the temple was destroyed.

Just as there were Jews back then that did believe, today there are many Hebrew saints with Jewish backgrounds that have received the Lord. We must be careful to cast off any proclivity to assess this nation based on a past generation that rejected the Messiah. God loves the Jewish people. They still have a covenant with God, and all Israel shall be saved (Romans 11:25–27). Let us celebrate and bless the nation of Israel and its people as being God's original instrument to bring the gospel of Christ to the world. God brings reformation when leaders become wicked and their systems or religious structures confine, control, or hold the masses of his people in bondage. It is God's will to activate each member within the body of Christ, not just a select few. Religion causes division and makes distinctions—clergy and laity, the rich and poor—similar to that of caste systems of the privileged and the disadvantaged, or White and Black; this was the spiritual climate at Azusa.

> History shows that Spiritual upgrade is revelatory and is established by the reformation of current revelation knowledge of recovered spiritual truth.

In 1906, the Azusa Street Revival crossed all racial boundaries in the middle of strict Jim Crow racial system of separation. God raised up a thirty-six-year-old apostle by the name of William Seamore, leader of the Apostolic Faith Mission. Seamore preached that it was God's will to fill people with the Holy Spirit, and God moved in an awesome way. From the alienated to the uneducated, every person was a participant in his meetings. People came from as far as China and India. It is reported that some who witnessed this outpouring say that the atmosphere of heaven came down to earth. This outpouring started with the poor, the castaways, the disadvantaged. It activated and brought the release of all believers from all walks of life an issue that some leaders fear because of the loss of control. According to the book of Joel, it is the will of God to baptize ALL flesh with his Holy Spirit to empower them with gifts of the Spirit (Joel 2:28). It is his will to teach and train the saints for the work of the ministry (Ephesians 4:11–12).

Strict segregation was the norm in America. In 1906, when there were more lynching of Black men than in any other year of America's history, Seymour led an interracial worship service. At Azusa Street, there were no preferences for age, gender, or race. One worshipper said, "The blood of Jesus washed the color line away."[28] It was common for the lost to be saved, sick healed, demonized delivered, and seekers to be baptized in the Spirit in almost every meeting. Many of the early leaders of the Pentecostal movement received their Holy Ghost baptism or worshipped at the Azusa "plank" altar. Because of this reformation of Spirit Baptism, today nearly six hundred million Pentecostal and Charismatic Christians around the world trace their roots back to this mighty outpouring of the Holy Spirit.

> And no man putteth new wine into old bottles;
> else the new wine will burst the bottles, and be
> spilled, and the bottles shall perish. But new wine
> must be put into new bottles; and both are pre-
> served. (Luke 5:37–38)

Today, we are in the midst of apostolic reform. It has gained great momentum both nationally and internationally. Recovered revelation knowledge is morphing the so-called church, causing a shift in leadership from the old pastoral to the new apostolic, from the pastor shepherd to the apostle pioneer; this shifting is causing the authentic *ekklesia* to emerge. This apostolic reformation contains the revelatory kingdom blueprint to construct the new wineskin for the outpouring and containment of new wine for the twenty-first and twenty-second-century *ekklesia*.

Anointing upon and within

Before we examine this reformation aspect, let us look at the foundational biblical purpose, two functions and the definition of anointing. Scripture first reveals that the act of anointing was the inaugural ceremony for priests. The root word of anointing is anoint. To anoint means to rub, pour, smear, or paint. It is in this act of anointing that the Holy Spirit is represented symbolically by oil for spiritual consecration and empowering an individual to stand in a particular office such as king, priest (Leviticus 8:12), or prophet under the old economy. This oil anointing is a type and shadow of the Holy Spirit. At this point, we should also note that in addition to the anointing *upon,* an anointing resides *within* every New Testament born-again believer. Conversely, there is an outer and an inner anointing. The anointing *upon* represents the supernatural ability of the Holy Spirit upon a human vessel for empowerment (Luke 4:18, Isaiah 42:1, Daniel 9:24). As indicated in the book of Acts, the anointing of the Holy Ghost empowered Jesus (as it does us) to heal sickness and deliver people from demonic oppression.

> How God anointed Jesus of Nazareth with the
> Holy Ghost and with power: who went about
> doing good, and healing all that were oppressed
> of the devil; for God was with him. (Acts 10:38)

Another word for the *anointing* is *unction*, found in 1 John 2:20–27. This is the word *chrisma* from the Greek word *khárisma.* This is the anointing within every born-again believer that guards against false teachers and imparts clarity of faith and judgment; this anointing is the truth, and it teaches believers to discern truth.

> But ye have an unction from the Holy One, and
> ye know all things. (1 John 2:20)

> But the anointing which ye have received of him
> abideth in you, and ye need not that any man

teach you: but as the same anointing teacheth
you of all things, and is truth, and is no lie, and
even as it hath taught you, ye shall abide in him.
(1 John 2:27)

Reformation anointing

See, I have this day set thee over the nations
and over the kingdoms, to root out, and to pull
down, and to destroy, and to throw down, to
build, and to plant. (Jeremiah 1:10)

The reformation anointing is by most standards a radical anointing. This anointing can be seen in the Old and New Testaments alike.

Samson—had a radical ministry.

And when he came unto Lehi, the Philistines
shouted against him: and the Spirit of the LORD
came mightily upon him, and the cords that were
upon his arms became as flax that was burnt with
fire, and his bands loosed from off his hands.
And he found a new jawbone of an ass, and put
forth his hand, and took it, and slew a thousand
men therewith. (Judges 15:14–15)

Jesus—had a radical ministry

And the Jews' Passover was at hand, and Jesus
went up to Jerusalem. And found in the temple
those that sold oxen and sheep and doves, and
the changers of money sitting: And when he had
made a scourge of small cords, he drove them all
out of the temple, and the sheep, and the oxen;
and poured out the changers' money, and over-

threw the tables; And said unto them that sold doves, Take these things hence; make not my Father's house an house of merchandise. (John 2:13–16)

Jehu—had a radical ministry

And he arose, and went into the house; and he poured the oil on his head, and said unto him, Thus saith the LORD God of Israel, I have anointed thee king over the people of the LORD, even over Israel. And thou shalt smite the house of Ahab thy master, that I may avenge the blood of all the servants the prophets, and the blood of all the servants of the LORD, at the hand of Jezebel. (2 Kings 9:6–7)

God sent Jesus into the world with a special commission. Jesus is the fulfillment of the new apostolic order; his mission is to fulfill the will and purpose of God.

The apostolic anointing brings to focus a particular type or unique quality that differentiates one type or flow or flavor of the anointing from another. Each ministry gift carries with it a particular anointing or anointing *blend*. Let me list a couple of the blended anointing we see in the church today. Apostolic teachers, prophetic teachers, etc.—that enables the servant of that office to fulfill God's purpose which is to perfect (bring to maturity) the believers in the Ekklesia which is Christ's body.

In researching the dictionary definition of the word apostolic, the basic definition found is that of or relating to or deriving from the apostles, their teaching, work, or time. *Apostolic* in the Noah Webster dictionary 1828 edition gives these descriptions: (1) pertaining or relating to apostles, as the apostolic age and (2) according to the doctrines of the apostles; delivered or taught by the apostles, as apostolic faith or practice. In order to understand this term fully, we will also examine the origin of the word *apostle*.

The first Christian apostles were Jewish men chosen from among the disciples who were "sent forth" (as indicated by the Greek word απόστολος, *apostolos,* or "messenger") by Jesus to preach the gospel to both Jews and Gentiles, across the then-known world.[29] And when it was day, he called unto him his disciples, and of them he chose twelve, whom also he named apostles (Luke 6:13). After praying all night, Jesus then launches an apostolic strategy for a new leadership order of ministry under the New Testament. In the Old Testament, the prophet is the primary messenger used by God to establish his righteousness and give direction to his people. The scripture says Jesus called unto his disciples, and of them, he chose twelve whom also he named apostles. Jesus did not name them evangelists, pastors, teachers, or even prophets. He named them apostles. This is New Testament reformation. The designation "apostle" is a New Testament enigma in its relationship to the Old Testament; it is baffling and cannot be explained by Old Testament theology, although we can now see Old Testament apostolic types. The full function and existence of this gift and office is not brought to manifestation until Jesus named, "onomazo," them apostles. This is a new kingdom order; it is a shift from the Old Testament prophetic order to the New Testament apostolic order. This is not too diminish the importance of the prophet but to upgrade the prophetic gift and office to New Testament order (Ephesians 4:11). The historical use of the term apostle is as a military expedition, and later it referred to a band of colonists sent overseas. According to the *Theological Dictionary of the New Testament* (Kittle) and the *Dictionary of New Testament Theology* (Brown), the word apostolos was originally used in maritime language to designate a "cargo vessel" or the fleet sent out on a military/colonizing expedition. Later it became the word used to refer to the commander of the invading/colonizing force, or to the group of colonists who were sent to "Hellenize" a region. The commission for all believers is to colo-

> "The apostolic extends beyond function and works, if you are born again; apostolic is who you are".

nize or disciple to bring the message and kingdom life to a dying world. To do this, we have been given power and the ability of overcoming the works of the devil.

> And Jesus came and spake unto them, saying, All power is given unto me in heaven and in earth. Go ye therefore, and teach all nations, baptizing them in the name of the Father, and of the Son, and of the Holy Ghost: Teaching them to observe all things whatsoever I have commanded you: and, lo, I am with you alway, even unto the end of the world. Amen. (Matthew 28:18–20)

The word *teach* is the word *matheteuo* {math-ayt-yoo'-o} from the Strongs concordance. It means to be a disciple and to make disciples to teach and instruct. These are definitions taken from the Strong's Concordance *matheteuo* (math-ayt-yoo'-o) from 3101(1) to be a disciple of one (1.a) to follow his precepts and instructions (2) 1551 to make a disciple, (2.a) to teach, instruct KJV: teach 2, instruct 1, be disciple 1. For further details, see Kittel's Theological Dictionary of the New Testament, 4:461, 552.

Apostolic prophetic dimension blend

> See, I have this day set thee over the nations and over the kingdoms, to root out, and to pull down, and to destroy, and to throw down, to build, and to plant. (Jeremiah 1:10)

The apostolic prophetic dimension is a blended dimension. It is a scope of the anointing that is indigenous to the New Testament apostle. Jesus functioned as a prophet under the Old Testament Law of Moses, while at the same time, he was anointed to execute and establish the office of the apostle who is both king, and our apostle and high priest (Hebrews 3:1). This blended dimension refers to the range or degree of grace to which the anointing extends in magnitude, size, and marked personality. This dimension also deals with one or more of the elements or factors that make up the persona, behavior, and appearance of this grace. The apostle Paul gave us insight into this dimension of grace when writing his second epistle to the church at Corinth.

> Truly the signs of an apostle were wrought among you in all patience, in signs, and wonders, and mighty deeds. (2 Corinthians 12:12)

Paul says that the signs, or we could say the marks, of an apostle had been wrought. *Wrought* or *katergazomai* means to perform, accomplish, achieve, or work. This was done among them in all patience. Here is a dimension of the apostolic that deserves our attention. First, let me say this: some in the church today see the apostolic office as one to be sought after and desired because of its perceived power, authority, or prestige. However, what they fail to see is the humiliation, digression, persecution, and suffering that come along with it. This is not a cup that most saints want to drink, nor do they want to be abused or persecuted. Yet the Bible teaches that the apostles and prophets are the substructure, the floor or foundation, of the house of God, walked on by the rest of the body of Christ. The church is built upon the foundation of these two grace gifts.

> Now therefore ye are no more strangers and foreigners, but fellowcitizens with the saints, and of the household of God; And are built upon the foundation of the apostles and prophets, Jesus Christ himself being the chief corner stone. (Ephesians 2:19–20)

A foundation is not something that is supported; rather, it is something that gives stability and support. The apostles and prophets are the Lord's groundwork and literal foundation in the house of God. Some want to be apostles, but very few want to be walked on.

If anyone had an insight into this realm (other than the Lord himself), it was the apostle Paul. This apostle visited the abode of God in the third heaven and heard things that were too holy to repeat (2 Corinthians 12:2–4). Paul had so much revelation concerning Christ and the church, that a messenger from Satan (called a thorn in the flesh in 2 Corinthians 12:7) was allowed to beat him so that he did not get lifted up in pride and miss the position God had for him in the kingdom. God used him to write most of the New Testament. Paul had revelation knowledge concerning the purpose and plan of God. However, it is important to note that today's view of the apostolic office and Paul's view is very different. Look at his thoughts concerning this:

> For I think that God hath set forth us the apostles last, as it were appointed to death: for we are made a spectacle unto the world, and to angels, and to men. We are fools for Christ's sake, but ye are wise in Christ; we are weak, but ye are strong; ye are honourable, but we are despised. Even unto this present hour we both hunger, and thirst, and are naked, and are buffeted, and have no certain dwellingplace; And labour, working with our own hands: being reviled, we bless; being persecuted, we suffer it: Being defamed, we intreat: we are made as the filth of the world, and are the offscouring of all things unto this day. (1 Corinthians 4:9–13)

Look at this translation from the New Testament, the contemporary language:

> It seems to me that God has put us who bear his Message on stage in a theater in which no one wants to buy a ticket. We're something everyone stands around and stares at, like an accident in the street. We're the Messiah's misfits. You might

be sure of yourselves, but we live in the midst of frailties and uncertainties. You might be well thought of by others, but we're mostly kicked around. Much of the time we don't have enough to eat, we wear patched and threadbare clothes, we get doors slammed in our faces, and we pick up odd jobs anywhere we can to eke out a living. When they call us names, we say, "God bless you." When they spread rumors about us, we put in a good word for them. We're treated like garbage, potato peelings from the culture's kitchen. And it's not getting any better. (1 Corinthians 4:9–13)

It is amazing that today, many see the honor, but few see the pain and price of suffering that come with the apostolic office. Look at what the Lord said about the apostle Paul's ministry.

But the Lord said unto him, Go thy way: he is a chosen vessel unto me, to bear my name before the Gentiles, and kings, and the children of Israel: For I will shew him how great things he must suffer for my name's sake. (Acts 9:15–16)

Scripture seems to conclude that what we call great ministry is in reality great suffering. In this country (United States), no one wants to go as far as to suffer—not to say that we should desire to suffer, because if we did, we would be sadistic. However, when it comes to Christ and the righteousness of God, we should not mind suffering if it will increase his glory, establish his will, and extend his kingdom. When we begin to think like this, we will soon get to the point that few Christians ever reach, the point to where we can rejoice in our suffering for his sake.

Long-suffering/forbearance

Patience corresponds with the fruit of the spirit called long-suffering, found in Galatians, the fifth chapter. Long-suffering is that patient endurance and steadfastness under ill will, that has no thought of retaliation. It is that quality of self-restraint which does not retaliate or punish. Long-suffering is the opposite of anger; it's associated with mercy and does not surrender to circumstances. Long-suffering is a character quality of God. In the seed form, patience grows in trials to yield the fruit of long-suffering that perfects the Christian character.

> My brethren, count it all joy when ye fall into divers temptations; Knowing this, that the trying of your faith worketh patience. But let patience have her perfect work, that ye may be perfect and entire, wanting nothing. (James 1:2–4)

Paul said that the signs of an apostle were worked, performed, accomplished, or achieved in all patience (long-suffering). The presence of this fruit speaks of forbearance, and inner strength, which is the foundational character quality of those that flow effectively in the apostolic office. The spiritual authority and sheer power of the anointing upon and within an individual that walks in this office must be tempered with the fruit of long-suffering and forbearance.

In writing to this church, the apostle pointed out the fact that there were thousands of instructors (teachers in the body of Christ that could point out their mistakes and their sins), but there were few fathers, those that were willing to take the time and effort to help them grow up spiritually in the gospel. As it is in the natural, so it is in the spiritual. There are many babies being born today in the natural, but there is not a lot of fathering that is going on, and God is not pleased. Any "of age" male can get together with any "of age" female (prayerfully his wife) and conceive a child. However, just because he helps in the conception of a baby, it does not automatically make him a father. It takes something more; it takes forbearance.

Forbearance is toleration, temperance, or restraint. (Not to be confused with compromise.) It literally means being able to put up with people and their mess (sin) while God brings them to maturity. Let me add that forbearance does not mean that you do not chasten spiritual children, for then they would be bastards (fatherless). There are so many sons and daughters in the body of Christ that have missed the mentoring of a spiritual father. A father who would forebear, allow them the grace to make mistakes without crushing them or destroying their zeal, and at the same time, firmly and lovingly chasten them. If a spiritual father is insensitive and harsh, he may minister hurt and harm rather than life and edification (2 Corinthians 10:8). Also see 1 Thessalonians 2:10–12.

Revelatory grace

Apostles not only lay the foundation of Christ; they inspect and test what is already laid, and because of the strength of their office, they can challenge a faulty premise, demolish it, and lay the proper truth. Apostles are not the type of people that you can just have a nice, surface-type of relationship with. The Lord has so gifted them to be people of depth you can always find them somewhere beneath the surface of a thing checking the substructure. Apostles are those that are so in love with truth, wisdom, and understanding that they are willing to dig for them if need be. They may seem intrusive, overbearing, or even noisy, but they are not; they are apostles, bottom-line people ordained by God to build the foundation and deal with the infrastructure of the church. The grace ability to digest deep and sometimes complicated, incomprehensible truth and then communicate it through teaching and preaching, in its simplest form, bringing illumination, revelation, and causing those that hear to see, is another aspect of the apostolic gift in operation.

> Unto me, who am less than the least of all saints,
> is this grace given, that I should preach among
> the Gentiles the unsearchable riches of Christ;
> And to make all men see what is the fellowship

of the mystery, which from the beginning of the world hath been hid in God, who created all things by Jesus Christ: To the intent that now unto the principalities and powers in heavenly places might be known by the church the manifold wisdom of God. (Ephesians 3:8–10)

<h1 style="text-align:center">5</h1>

Israel-Advanced Technologies

Growing up as a child I remember watching the cartoon show called *The Jetsons*, produced by Hanna Barbera. The Jetsons was the twenty-first-century version of *The Flintstones* but did not do as well in the ratings and was canceled after its first season. It was then grouped with other cartoons (*The Flintstones* and *Jonny Quest*) to become a strong Saturday morning attraction. George Jetson, his wife, Jane, daughter, Judy, and son, Elroy, lived in a technologically advanced world. At that time, they represented the portrait of the future of technology. With flying cars that folded up in to suitcases, moving sidewalks, robots that did the housecleaning and telephones with pictures, it was "videoconferencing" before anyone had even coined the term. Today, we do not have any practical flying cars, and we still have to deal with traffic and parking issues; however, in airports today, you can find moving sidewalks, we do have robots that can be programmed to keep the floors clean around the house, and, thanks to the latest release from Apple, we have wireless video conferencing in the palm of our hands. The things that seemed far-fetched back then are commonplace today. Just think, if you had access to twenty-first-century technology in the eighteenth century, you would become very powerful, perhaps very wealthy very quickly. In the natural realm, technology is birth through the scientific discovery of knowledge, but in the spirit realm, it is revelation knowledge that gives supernatural breakthrough. Just as there are still natural discoveries yet to be discovered that will lead to breakthroughs in the natural realm, there are spiritual technologies and strategies yet to be released to the church. The Bible teaches that God has stored up hidden wisdom for our glory. This wisdom is hidden for us, not from us, and is revealed to us by the Holy Spirit (1 Corinthians 2:7–10). The Spirit of God can even give wisdom for natural inventions.

> I wisdom dwell with prudence, and find out knowledge of witty inventions. (Proverbs 8:12)

King Uzziah

We see an example of this in the life of King Uzziah. The King James Version says he made in Jerusalem engines, invented by cunning men (2 Chronicles 26:15). *Engine* is from the word *chishshabown*, which means a warlike machine. For Uzziahs's day, this was advanced, cutting-edge technology. Here is the translation from *The Message* Bible.

> Uzziah had them well-armed with shields, spears, helmets, armor, bows, and slingshots. He also installed the latest in military technology on the towers and corners of Jerusalem for shooting arrows and hurling stones. He became well known for all this—a famous king. (2 Chronicles 26:14–15)

The technology of running water

During the nineteenth century, women in childbirth were dying at alarming rates in Europe and the United States. Up to 25 percent of women who delivered their babies in hospitals died from childbed fever (puerperal sepsis), later found to be caused by *Streptococcus pyogenes bacteria.* As early as 1843, Dr. Oliver Wendell Holmes advocated hand washing to prevent childbed fever. Holmes was horrified by the prevalence in American hospitals of the fever, which he believed to be an infectious disease passed to pregnant women by the hands of doctors.[30] In 1845, a young doctor in Vienna named Dr. Ignaz Semmelweis was horrified at the terrible death rate of women who gave birth in hospitals. As many as 30 percent died after giving birth. Semmelweis noted that doctors would examine the bodies of patients who died, then, without washing their hands, go straight to the next ward and examine expectant mothers. This was their normal practice, because the presence of microscopic diseases was unknown. Semmelweis insisted that doctors wash their hands before examinations, and the death rate immediately dropped 2 percent.[31] Two percent may not seem like much, but when it comes to human life, this is a tremendous advancement. While these two doctors had stumbled upon the cause of this medical disaster, they had yet to come to the complete solution to this medical tragedy. Centuries before the invention of the microscope, God protected his people from microscopic germs and diseases that could not be seen with the naked eye. God's people never suffered from this type of tragic accidental death brought on by ignorance, because God gave his people algorithms and exact instructions to deal with infectious diseases. The book of Leviticus records the technology of running water.

> And when he that has an issue is cleansed of his
> issue; then he shall number to himself even days
> for his cleansing, and wash his clothes, and bathe
> his flesh in running water, and shall be clean.
> (Leviticus 15:13)

Until recent years, doctors washed their hands in a bowl of water, leaving invisible germs on their hands. However, the Bible says specifically to bathe the flesh in "running water," and it shall be clean. This is a simple technology, yet because of a lack of knowledge, many people lost their life needlessly. Today, this simple technology that can mean the difference of life or death in patient care has been implemented in hospitals around the world (https://www.

britannica.com/biography/Ignaz-Semmelweis Zoltán, Imre. "Ignaz Semmelweis." Encyclopedia Britannica, 9 Aug. 2020, https://www. britannica.com/biography/Ignaz-Semmelweis. Accessed 8 February 2021).

Quarantine technologies

Fred Williams points out that in numerous instances, the Bible contains medical information that far predates man's actual discoveries of related principles in the field of medicine. The medical instructions given by Moses to the Israelites some 3,500 years ago were not only far superior to the practices of contemporary cultures; they also exceeded medical standards practiced as recently as one hundred years ago. Where did Moses get this advanced information? Following are some examples of the medical knowledge afforded the Israelites in biblical times.

Sanitary practices. For centuries, doctors denied the possibility that disease could be transmitted by invisible agents. However, in the late nineteenth century, Louis Pasteur demonstrated in his germ theory of disease that most infectious diseases were caused by microorganisms originating from outside the body. This new understanding of germs and their means of transmission led to improved sanitary standards that resulted in an enormous drop in the mortality rate. Yet these core principles of sanitation were being practiced by the Israelites thousands of years earlier. The Israelites were instructed to wash themselves and their clothes in running water if they came in contact with a dead body, if they came in contact with another person's discharge, or if they had touched a dead human or animal carcass. They were also instructed to wash any uncovered vessels that were in the vicinity of a dead body, and if a dead carcass touched a vessel, it was to be destroyed. Items recovered during war were also to be purified through either fire or running water. In addition, the Israelites were instructed to bury their human waste outside of camp, and to burn the waste of their animals (see Numbers 19, Leviticus

11 and 15, Deuteronomy 23:12). These sanitary practices, without question, saved countless lives in the Israelite camps by protecting them against infection caused by unseen germs. Meanwhile, their Egyptian peers were dying by the thousands due to "remedies" that almost always consisted of some amount of human or animal dung.[32] As mentioned earlier, the sound sanitary practices that we take for granted today only began to flourish about a hundred years ago.

Bacteria. Sometime after I wrote these web pages, a Bible skeptic unwittingly showed me yet another example of advanced scientific/ medical knowledge in the Bible. He posted a message on a discussion board that ridiculed some verses in Leviticus 13 and 14 that mention leprosy on walls and on garments. He felt this was silly and an error since leprosy is a human disease. What this skeptic was unaware of is the fact that leprosy is a bacteria, a living organism, that certainly can survive on walls and garments! In fact, the Medic-Planet.com encyclopedia notes that leprosy "can survive three weeks or longer outside the human body, such as in dust or on clothing."[33] It is no wonder that God commanded the Levitical priests to burn the garments of leprosy victims! (Leviticus 13:52)

Laws of quarantine. In the same Med-Planet encyclopedia cited above, we read that "it was not until 1873 that leprosy could be shown to be infectious rather than hereditary."[34] Of course, God knew this all along, as His laws to Moses reveal (Leviticus 13, 14, 22; Numbers 19:20). His instructions regarding quarantine to prevent the spread of leprosy and other infectious diseases are nothing short of remarkable, considering that this lifesaving practice was several thousand years ahead of its time. Infected persons were instructed to isolate themselves outside the camp until healed, and were to shave and wash thoroughly. The priests that administered care were instructed to change their clothes and wash thoroughly after inspecting a plague victim.

It should be reemphasized that the Israelites were the only culture to practice quarantine until the last century, when medical advances finally demonstrated the importance of sanitation and isolation during plagues. The devastating black plague of the fourteenth century that claimed millions of lives was not broken until the church fathers in Vienna began encouraging the public to start following the guidelines as set forth in the Bible. The promising results in Vienna compelled other cities to follow suit, and the dreaded plague was finally eradicated.[3]

The first antiseptic. Hyssop oil was charged by God to Moses to be used as a purifying agent. Hyssop oil has been shown to contain 50 percent antifungal and antibacterial agents (Numbers 19:18, Psalms 51:7).

Circumcision and blood clotting. For centuries, scholars must have been perplexed by God's law of circumcision which required the procedure to be performed on the 8th day after birth (Genesis 17:12, Genesis 21:14, Leviticus 12:3, Luke 2:21). Medical researchers recently discovered that the two main blood-clotting factors, vitamin K and prothrombin, reach their highest level in life, about 110 percent of normal, on the eighth day after birth. These blood-clotting agents facilitate rapid healing and greatly reduce the chance of infection. You can verify with any obstetrician that the eighth day of life is the ideal time for a circumcision, and that any circumcision done earlier requires an injection of vitamin K supplement.

Dietary guidelines. By the 1980s, all the health organizations of the United States had adopted low-fat, high-fiber dietary guidelines. This was the culmination of numerous scientific studies that had demonstrated that diets high in vegetables, fruits, and grains reduced the risk of heart disease, cancer, and many other diseases. Secular physicians generally agree that these dietary guidelines that were producing longer life spans were first developed by religious movements founded in the 1800s, particularly by the Seventh-Day Adventists. Where did the Seventh-Day Adventists get their guidelines? From a meticulous and careful study of the Bible.[4] It appears man has finally caught up to the dietary recommendations given by God to the Israelites some 3,500 years ago!

6

Technology of Oneness

How can people be on one accord except in a spirit of prayer? Oneness in the church is accomplished in prayer. One Lord, one faith, one baptism. It is the Lord who uses prayer to bring his body in unison with his plan, purpose, and move of his Spirit. Oneness, not just unity, is such a powerful technology of the Spirit. This algorithm works for the saved and unsaved alike. Even Satan himself uses fear to unite his demonic hordes forcing them to keep their ranks because a kingdom divided against itself cannot stand (Luke 11:17–18). I believe the Lord will use this principle of oneness to mobilize the body of Christ simultaneously around the world, casting out devils, healing the sick, raising the dead, giving sight to the blind, and preaching the gospel of the kingdom, accomplishing his will on a global scale (Mathew 24:14). The restrictions imposed on Jesus by incarnation have been removed; and because of this, in the coming days, we will witness the greater works of corporate Christ moving in unison and total oneness (John 14:12). The church will become one because Jesus prayed that we would be one even as he and the Father are one. The technology of oneness releases a supernatural power that reaches beyond comprehension. It is the power to literally do what is literally impossible. Oneness is much different than unity; people can decide to unite for a common purpose yet have different agenda and still not be one. The technology of oneness is so powerful that there is one incident in the Bible where the Lord had to leave the heavens and come to earth to stop the progress of a people who not only were working in unity. They had tapped into this power technology of oneness; nothing could restrain them because the people had become one.

> And they said one to another, Go to, let us make brick, and burn them thoroughly. And they had brick for stone, and slime had they for morter. And they said, Go to, let us build us a city and a tower, whose top may reach unto heaven; and let us make us a name, lest we be scattered abroad upon the face of the whole earth. And the LORD came down to see the city and the tower, which the children of men builded. And the LORD said, Behold, the people is one, and they have all one language; and this they begin to do: and now nothing will be restrained from them, which they have imagined to do. Go to, let us go down, and there confound their language, that they may not understand one another's speech. So the LORD scattered them abroad from thence upon the face of all the earth: and they left off to build the city. (Genesis 11:3–8)

Apostolic technologies and algorithms

> And he said unto them, Go ye into all the world, and preach the gospel to every creature. He that believeth and is baptized shall be saved; but he that believeth not shall be damned. And these signs shall follow them that believe; In my name shall they cast out devils; they shall speak with new tongues; They shall take up serpents; and if they drink any deadly thing, it shall not hurt

> them; they shall lay hands on the sick, and they
> shall recover. (Mark 16:15–18)

Jesus ministered as a prophet under the old economy. Here, he gives his disciples an apostolic command. This is an apostolic strategy to accomplish the will of God to reach the world with the gospel. It is not just a command to the twelve but to all disciples. Jesus is the mature manifestation of the prophetic word that God spoke to the serpent in the garden after the fall of man. In Genesis 3:15, God prophesied about a warring seed that would bruise the serpent's head. Jesus is that apostolic seed; the "sent one"; the Greek word *apostolos,* meaning messenger.

> And I will put enmity between thee and the
> woman, and between thy seed and her seed; it
> shall bruise thy head, and thou shalt bruise his
> heel. (Genesis 3:15)

> As they ministered to the Lord, and fasted, the
> Holy Ghost said, Separate me Barnabas and
> Saul for the work whereunto I have called them.
> And when they had fasted and prayed, and laid
> their hands on them, they sent them away. (Acts
> 13:2–3)

Antioch is a church that was born out of persecution, and it is at Antioch that we see a clear pattern and prototype of a functional apostolic New Testament church guided by the Holy Spirit yet still in its infancy. This is an important point to understand because the pattern or picture of this church in the book of Acts is not yet fully developed. Just as a baby must go through stages of growth—becoming a young child, then teenager to adult corporate Christ (Ephesians 4:11–16)—this is also true of the Antioch church (Acts 13:1). Some leaders have attempted to incorporate pieces of the Antioch pattern and built churches that are incomplete of the full revelation. Case in point, the Antioch pattern cannot reach its true New Testament-kingdom potential without genuine plurality of leadership and the set foundation of apostles first. Leaders who reject this established order will build churches that resemble and function as cults. Let's look briefly at the definition of a cult: followers of an unorthodox, extremist, or false religion or sect who often live outside of conventional society under the direction of a charismatic leader; a religion or sect that is generally considered to be unorthodox, extremist, or false.

> And God hath set some in the church, first apostles, secondarily prophets, thirdly teachers, after that miracles, then gifts of healings, helps, governments, diversities of tongues. (1 Corinthians 12:28)

Ministering to the Lord and fasting

One of the lost skills being restored to the church is ministering to the Lord. Ministering to the Lord while fasting is an act of extreme adoration and love. For the most part, this extreme worship is missing in our churches because it seems that saints do not have a deeply intimate relationship with the Lord; their first love has been hijacked by religion and the tradition of men. Leaving your first love does not mean you have left Jesus entirely; it means that he is no longer first or central in your life.

> Nevertheless I have somewhat against thee, because thou hast left thy first love. (Revelation 2:4)

Our Christian life is a life of warfare against sin, Satan, the world, our self-life, and the flesh. We must never yield to our spiritual enemies; if we do, we resign ourselves to a life of bondage; therefore, we must fight to keep our first love vibrant.

It takes a deep sincere love for the Lord to minister to him while denying oneself with fasting (Luke 9:23). On the other hand, it is lust that comes to take all it can. Meaning, that many lust for what the Lord can give them, rather than loving him for who he is.

God is a personal being, and it gives him great pleasure to have other beings he can have a genuine relationship with. We were created for God's pleasure and so we could experience the pleasure of knowing him. For many, religion and tradition have stripped them away from their relationship with God. Many have the mindset that it is the Lord's job to bless and minister to them, yet it is the Lord who is worthy of our adoration, blessing, and praise; this is *our* ministry to him.

Also, it takes time to minister to the Lord. Ministering and waiting before the Lord has become a lost art. Waiting before the Lord is something that many times has not been factored into many of today's church services.

> But they that wait upon the LORD shall renew
> [their] strength; they shall mount up with wings
> as eagles; they shall run, and not be weary; [and]
> they shall walk, and not faint. (Isaiah 40:31)

Ministering to him with songs of thanksgiving (Psalms 69:30–31) and waiting on the Lord in this modern day seems to be a thing of the past (Isaiah 40:31).

In many traditional services where they program two fast songs and one slow or various choir selections which do not take into account the flow of the Holy Spirit, these services, many times, amount to nothing more than flesh on parade. Remember, the scripture says, "God is a Spirit: and they that worship him must worship him in spirit and in truth" (John 4:24). Also, some church services are bound by time restraints to finish one service so that the next can begin. We must move away from this mechanized substitute and return to the true biblical patten of praise, worship, and glory. Ruth Heflin, in her book *Glory: Experiencing the Atmosphere of Heaven*, says, "We must praise until the spirit of worship comes then worship until the glory comes then stand in the glory."[35] Our goal in gathering together should focus on entering into a heartfelt love and intimacy with the Holy Spirit because true intimacy with the Lord cannot be rushed, it cannot be manufactured, and it most certainly cannot be faked.

Entering God's presence cannot be defined by a religious routine. In a relationship, we naturally expect there to be a response from both parties. If there is no exchange from both parties, there is no relationship; the same applies to God. For example, ministering to the Lord with fasting and prayer was practices by the Antioch church (Acts 13:2–3). In their gatherings, time was given to allow the prophetic word to distill and then be uttered through the mouths of the prophets. The prophetic voices must be allowed to speak in *our* gatherings. The Lord cannot correct, teach, direct, or comfort his people unless the prophets are allowed to speak (see 2 Chronicles 20).

> Let the prophets speak two or three, and let the other judge. If any thing be revealed to another that sitteth by, let the first hold his peace. For ye may all prophesy one by one, that all may learn, and all may be comforted. And the spirits of the prophets are subject to the prophets. (1 Corinthians 14:29–32)

Antioch was a church that ministered to the Lord with fasting. It is a church that fasted and prayed. Let us not intermingle or confuse the two as being one. They are two separate algorithms that yield to separate and distinct output values. The input value algorithms of these spiritual technologies yielded these two output values:

Input-Output Values

Input Value 1: Ministering to the Lord and fasting
Output Value: Hearing the voice and instructions of the Holy Spirit
Input Value 2: Fasting and Prayer

Yielded Output Value: Setting apart for special tasks with laying on of hands

Among the leadership at Antioch were prophets and teachers. The utterance of the Holy Spirit, "Separate me Barnabas and Saul for the work whereunto I have called them" most likely came by prophecy through one of the prophets; this shows us the importance of the prophetic ministry and office of the prophet in the local church. This church gives us a portrait view and reveals the algorithms activated by these disciples and the technology used by the Holy Spirit, to identify and deploy the apostles (sent ones) Barnabas and Saul.

The implementation of these technologies gave this apostolic company the ability to press in and hear God's will, plan, and purpose. I am also persuaded to believe that the execution of these technologies had a transcending effect upon the fellowship in that these saints personified Christ, becoming the first to be recognized as "Christians" (Acts 11:26). Ministering to the Lord and fasting, fasting and prayer, and laying on of hands are all apostolic technologies.

Technology of laying on of hands

> And in those days, when the number of the disciples was multiplied, there arose a murmuring of the Grecians against the Hebrews, because their widows were neglected in the daily ministration. (Acts 6:1)

Here we see that a problem has developed within the congregation of the early church. Up until this point, the disciples have been walking in the unity of the Spirit (Ephesians 4:3) on one accord, now we see the bond of peace is being threatened. The scripture says that the Grecians (Greek-speaking Christians) started murmuring against the Hebrews (Aramaic-speaking Christians). A strife was developing because it appeared that preferential treatment was being shown in the allocation of food to the Hebrew widows. It may seem small, yet this is a serious problem. Strife can be deadly (James 3:16). It can cause a breach in fellowship and short-circuit the anointing in a church. I want to look in detail as to how the apostles used spiritual technologies and supernatural algorithms to solve this crisis. In my introduction, I gave you the definition of an algorithm. Let's rehearse it again. An algorithm is a precise, step-by-step plan for a computational procedure that begins with an input value and yields an output value in a finite number of steps. It is a precise rule (or set of rules) specifying how to solve some problem. Let's look at the problem. And in those days, when the number of the disciples was multiplied—it seems that the early church is having what we could call growing pains. Disciples were not just being added to the church; it says that their numbers were being multiplied. They were experiencing exponential growth. The fellowship was literally outgrowing its leadership.

Then the twelve called the multitude of the disciples unto them, and said, It is not reason that we should leave the word of God, and serve tables. Wherefore, brethren, look ye out among you seven men of honest report, full of the Holy Ghost and wisdom, whom we may appoint over this business. But we will give ourselves continually to prayer, and to the ministry of the word. And the saying pleased the whole multitude: and they chose Stephen, a man full of faith and of the Holy Ghost, and Philip, and Prochorus, and Nicanor, and Timon, and Parmenas, and Nicolas a proselyte of Antioch: Whom they set before the apostles: and when they had prayed, they laid their hands on them. And the word of God increased; and the number of the disciples multiplied in Jerusalem greatly; and a great company of the priests were obedient to the faith. (Acts 6:2–7)

We first see this concept of laying on of hands introduced with the laws of sacrifice and atonement or the covering of sin under the old economy. The worshipper bringing the sin offering would press their hand upon the animal's head. The intent was to symbolically show the physical and mental energy involved in the transfer of their sin into the life of the animal before it was killed and its blood sprinkled on the altar to atone for sin (Leviticus 1:4). In the book of Acts, the above scripture shows us that the seven men chosen by the congregation were approved and appointed to their office with the laying on of hands by the apostles. Laying on of hands is also used to minister the gift of the Holy Spirit (Acts 8:17, Acts 19:6) and healing the sick (Mark 16:18, Acts 28:8, Luke 13:13). This custom of laying on of hands was also practiced by the early patriarchs (Genesis 48:13–15) as a means of transferring *the blessing* from one generation to another. In Numbers 27:18–20, God told Moses to put some of his honor upon Joshua, i.e., publicly laying hands and transferring some of his authority upon Joshua that all the congregation of the children of Israel may be obedient. Also read Numbers 11:14–17 to see how God deployed the principal of plurality of leadership when Moses became overwhelmed by the burden of single-handedly ministering to the wilderness church.

7

Apostolic Career

*For the weapons of our warfare are not carnal, but mighty
through God to the pulling down of strongholds casting down
imaginations, and every high thing that exalteth itself against
the knowledge of God, and bringing into captivity every
thought to the obedience of Christ; And having in a readiness
to revenge all disobedience, when your obedience is fulfilled.*
—2 Corinthians 10:4–6

The word warfare in this scripture comes from the Greek word *strateia* which mean an expedition, a military campaign pertaining to military service; it means apostolic career. The Greek word for apostle is *apostolos*. In ancient times *apostolos* referred to a naval fleet carrying supplies that was sent out for a mission (Kittle).

In Exodus 15:3, scripture reveals God as a man of war. Over 230 times throughout the Old Testament, he is identified as "the Lord of Host." This name is used nearly three times more than any other name in the Bible. The word host translates from the word *tsaba,'* which is a mass of persons especially organized for war (an army). Our God is the Lord of the armies of heaven. Timothy was told to endure hardness, as a good soldier of Jesus Christ (2 Timothy 2:3). Apostolic people are warriors submitted to the Lord of hosts, who is a man of war (Exodus 15:3) also see (Isaiah 42:13). Waging war against the forces of darkness is our apostolic career. If you ask the question,

Why did Jesus come to earth suffered and died on the cross, many would say that he came to save them from going to hell. Still, others would say he came to die for their sin. While these answers do point out the benefits we receive as a result of his obedience to die on the cross, they don't give the major reason for his coming.

> For this purpose the Son of God was manifested, that he might destroy the works of the devil. (1 John 3:8)

The word apostle comes from a Greek word that means a dispatch of ships, a naval military operation.

> The LORD hath opened his armoury, and hath brought forth the weapons of his indignation: for this is the work of the Lord GOD of hosts in the land of the Chaldeans. (Jeremiah 50:25)

Christ Jesus, the apostle and high priest of our profession was sent and anointed by God to destroy the works of the devil. He was on a mission. He sent his disciples out on the same mission.

> And he called unto him the twelve, and began to send them forth by two and two; and gave them power over unclean spirits. (Mark 6:7)

Jesus sent the seventy out on the same mission.

> And as ye go, preach, saying, The kingdom of heaven is at hand. Heal the sick, cleanse the lepers, raise the dead, cast out devils: freely ye have received, freely give. (Matthew 10:7–8)

> And he said unto them, Go ye into all the world, and preach the gospel to every creature. He that believeth and is baptized shall be saved; but he

that believeth not shall be damned. And these
signs shall follow them that believe; In my name
shall they cast out devils; they shall speak with
new tongues; They shall take up serpents; and
if they drink any deadly thing, it shall not hurt
them; they shall lay hands on the sick, and they
shall recover. (Mark 16:15–18)

King David is an Old Testament apostolic type. He functioned
under a priestly, kingly, and prophetic anointing. David knew how
to release mercy as a priest, how to bring justices and judgment as a
king, and how to release his faith and the word of the Lord through
the prophetic anointing. David served as an officer in Israel's military
prior to becoming king; he was a man familiar with warfare.

And it was told king David, saying, The LORD
hath blessed the house of Obededom, and all
that pertaineth unto him, because of the ark of
God. So David went and brought up the ark of
God from the house of Obededom into the city
of David with gladness. (2 Samuel 6:12)

When David brought back the Ark of the Covenant, the presence of the Lord returned. David had a company of priests that ministered before the Lord continually (1 Chronicles 13–16, Psalms 149,
2 Samuel 6) from his stronghold in Zion (a type of church; a place
of prayer, praise, and worship). In this atmosphere of prayer, praise,
and worship, David was able to inquire of the Lord. The wisdom and
supernatural strategies he obtained gave him the ability to launch
apostolic raids to defeat his enemies, take land, and establish territory
for the kingdom of God. King David was a worshiping warrior with
a breakthrough anointing; he knew the Lord as the Lord of host.
Although he seemingly fought all his battles in the natural, David
walked in New Testament revelation under the Old Testament economy; he always had an edge because he knew how to tap into the

supernatural realm using the name of the Lord and the sword of the Spirit to prophesy and decree his enemies' defeat.

> Then said David to the Philistine, Thou comest to me with a sword, and with a spear, and with a shield: but I come to thee in the name of the LORD of hosts, the God of the armies of Israel, whom thou hast defied… And all this assembly shall know that the LORD saveth not with sword and spear: for the battle is the LORD's and he will give you into our hands. (1 Samuel 17:45, 47)

David had a recognizable relationship with the Lord; he was what I call a radical worshipper. This type of worship and praise has no shame; it confuses the enemy (2 Chronicles 20:22) and can drive the carnal mind to a point of disdain (2 Samuel 6:14–16). As commander in chief, David knew the importance of intelligence and counterintelligence in warfare. He knew how to access the wisdom of God; by asking in prayer, he inquired of the Lord.

> The Philistines also came and spread themselves in the valley of Rephaim. And David enquired of the LORD, saying, Shall I go up to the Philistines? Wilt thou deliver them into mine hand? And the LORD said unto David, Go up: for I will doubtless deliver the Philistines into thine hand. (2 Samuel 5:18–19)

To inquire means to seek information by questioning, or to make an investigation to seek to learn by asking. David kept a fresh relationship with the Lord and continued to seek his counsel. He didn't take anything for granted. David did not assume that his prior victory ensured him of success against the Philistines when they came up against him a second time. He was consistent in inquiring of the Lord, and by doing so, the Lord gave him supernatural offensive tactics to defeat the enemy.

> And the Philistines came up yet again, and spread themselves in the valley of Rephaim. And when David enquired of the LORD, he said, Thou shalt not go up; but fetch a compass behind them, and come upon them over against the mulberry trees. And let it be, when thou hearest the sound of a going in the tops of the mulberry trees, that then thou shalt bestir thyself: for then shall the LORD go out before thee, to smite the host of the Philistines. And David did so, as the LORD had commanded him; and smote the Philistines from Geba until thou come to Gazer. (2 Samuel 5:22–25)

> And David dwelt in the castle; therefore they called it the city of David. And he built the city round about, even from Millo round about: and Joab repaired the rest of the city. So David waxed greater and greater: for the LORD of hosts was with him. (1 Chronicles 11:7–9)

Some leaders miss the move

> No man also having drunk old wine straightway desireth new: for he saith, The old is better. (Luke 5:39)

Just as it was with first-century Israel, the religious leaders, Pharisees, and Sadducees (bound by religious spirits and the traditions of men) resisted and fought against the shift from Judaism (the old wineskin) to the church; there are some leaders today who are missing the current move of God because they refuse to embrace apostolic reform and upgrade their mindset of structure in ministry. The new wine of the Holy Spirit cannot be contained or function within the old denominational system which represents the religious mechanism of the conventional, modern-day church.

Spirit of control in the church

> I wrote unto the church: but Diotrephes, who loveth to have the preeminence among them, receiveth us not. Wherefore, if I come, I will remember his deeds which he doeth, prating against us with malicious words: and not content therewith, neither doth he himself receive the brethren, and forbiddeth them that would, and casteth them out of the church. (3 John 1:9–10)

> No man also having drunk old wine straight-way desireth new: for he saith, The old is better. (Luke 5:39)

Many leaders in this nation and around the world have or are in the process of making the shift from pastoral to apostolic (read Apostle John Eckhardt's *A Shift in Leadership*). However, there is also a resistance against apostolic reformation in churches where leaders, because of their insecurity, rejection, pride, and fear of losing their position, seek to perpetuate the old and control God's people within the religious system of denominationalism under the now-defunct pastoral model. These churches are kenspeckled by their legalistic and dogmatic practices; they are marked by a loss of liberty.

> Now the Lord is that Spirit: and where the Spirit of the Lord is, there is liberty. (2 Corinthians 3:17)

Initially, these churches may seem healthy; however, further examination will reveal that the leading of the Holy Spirit has been replaced by a spirit of control and witchcraft. The conviction of the

Holy Spirit is replaced by a spirit of guilt and condemnation. The anointing of the Holy Spirit is replaced by man's wisdom. Rather than life, there is death (2 Corinthians 3:6), accompanied by an overall sense of bondage. Although the leadership of the said church may claim to believe in healing and deliverance, there is very little, if any, real ministry to the saints. It is a church with a semblance of godliness that denies the power thereof (2 Timothy 3:5).

> And my speech and my preaching was not with enticing words of man's wisdom, but in demonstration of the Spirit and of power: That your faith should not stand in the wisdom of men, but in the power of God. (1 Corinthians 2:4)

Deliverance is replaced by counseling, which yields little results and no effect in destroying the forces of darkness in the lives of God's people. These churches are obtuse, anemic, void of spiritual life and power. Apostles and apostolic leadership are concerned about an individual's destiny and have no need to keep God's people under their personal control. I believe that most true apostles have been accused of being too radical when it comes to deliverance, but let's face it—deliverance is a radical ministry. It was radical when Jesus did it, and it's radical today. I understand some leaders don't want to rock the boat; however, this plays into the hand of the enemy, and this is the very posture that the enemy wants you to take. You can pretend the demons are not there. Yes, you can pretend, but that's all it will be is pretend, because demons will not go away just because you close your eyes and mind to their existence, no more than roaches will leave your house just because you chose to ignore them. Just as there is no substitute for exterminating your home, THERE IS NO SUBSTITUTE FOR DELIVERANCE IN THE CHURCH. Just as roaches must be exterminated, demons must be cast out. You cannot counsel demons, you cannot train demons, you cannot educate demons, you cannot reform demons, and you cannot redeem demons. They will always act out their demonic sinful nature; therefore, the only thing you can do is what Jesus did—cast them out! It is better to rock the boat getting a few people wet to get the devils out of the church than to build on a demonic foundation. Whatever you compromise to keep, you will eventually lose. Leaders who compromise in this area of deliverance are literally building on sand. This is one of the reasons that the kingdom was taken from the Jews. The Jewish leaders had kingdom authority to minister to God's convent people, but they abused their authority. They had no fruits that demonstrated that the kingdom even existed; they were more concerned with their own personal objectives and traditions than they were with executing and demonstrating a kingdom culture.

> Therefore say I unto you, The kingdom of God shall be taken from you, and given to a nation bringing forth the fruits thereof. (Matthew 21:43)

Personally, I do not believe a true servant of God would intentionally operate in control or witchcraft; nevertheless, I have found that these spirits are still active in the church today.

> But I fear, lest by any means, as the serpent beguiled Eve through his subtilty, so your minds should be corrupted from the simplicity that is in Christ. (2 Corinthians 11:3)

The verb *beguiled* represents the compound word *exapatao* which conveys the idea of utter or complete deception. So the question is, Can we be deceived? The evil behind deception is that you do not know you are deceived. The scriptural answer is yes. If you are not flowing in the discernment of the Holy Spirit, you can be deceived.

For the record, let me say this, no one has a right to control others! God gave free will to all, and even he will not seek to control you, nor will he violate your freewill. When anyone seeks to control a person or circumstance surrounding a person, they are actually entering into agreement with Satan and his demons. Any attempt an individual makes to control others becomes a practice of witchcraft! Witchcraft is the practice of controlling others for personal gain. Witchcraft is a work of the flesh, according to Galatians 5:19–21. Charismatic witchcraft is exercising control over other Christians by leaders or anyone within the church. Charismatic witches use personal prophecy to control others. Some of these witches or so-called prophets only prophesy about money, claiming to be prophets of God and calling themselves spiritual financial advisors. Like Balaam (Numbers 22), they are prophets for profit. Beloved, this is not of God.

I am a witness to this happening in the church. Several years ago, an elder explained to me a problem they had with another individual he and the other elders had welcomed to their church. This individual was very charismatic and claimed to be a prophet. The problem they were having in the congregation was that this prophet was giving people in the church private prophecies, and the prophecies seemed always centered around money. He prophesied to one man that his wife would die if he did not give him five thousand dollars.

In the spirit of love, the elders of the church confronted this man. They asked him to sit under the teaching of the church for one year and not to prophesy to anyone in the church, and afterward, they would release him to minister. These elders were doing exactly what they were called to do in guarding the sheep. This individual responded in writing, in short, saying that he did not need the elders of the church to start his ministry and that he would leave and start his own church. He refused to submit to the authority God placed in the church for his safety.

Where no counsel is, the people fall: but in the multitude of counsellors, there is safety (Proverbs 11:14).

A few years later, I went back to the elder and asked about this brother who left to start his own church. His response was, "None of the people who have gone to that church and left that church lives were any better." This elder became somewhat of a safety net for people whose lives were destroyed as a result of their membership in that church. I myself have counseled and ministered deliverance to people bound by witchcraft and strong spirits of control who were swindled out of large sums of money by the leader of that church. I personally have reached out to this leader and discussed his bondage. He agreed with me about the things the Holy Spirit had revealed to me about his life, but to this day, he has refused deliverance.

> Feed the flock of God which is among you,
> taking the oversight thereof, not by constraint,
> but willingly; not for filthy lucre, but of a ready
> mind; Neither as being lords over God's heritage,
> but being ensamples to the flock. (1 Peter 5:2–3)

The word *lords* in the scripture above is the Greek word *katakurieuo* (kat-ak-oo-ree-yoo'-o), which means to bring under one's power, to subject one's self, to subdue, master, to hold in subjection, to be master of, exercise lordship over. In the King James version of the Bible, it means to: exercise dominion over, overcome, be lord over, exercise lordship over. Since we believe that no one would knowingly practice witchcraft nor control in the church, how does this happen? One of the ways witchcraft works through leaders is through past bondage from which they have never received deliverance. Things the enemy attached to them during their childhood, one such spirit is rejection. I believe King Saul suffered from rejection. Saul wanted acceptance from people more than from God. Saul feared that the people would reject him, and this drove him to commit twisted acts of disobedience toward God. Note the spirit of rejection assembles a threefold demonic link consisting of rejection, fear of rejection, and self-rejection.

> And Saul said unto Samuel, I have sinned: for
> I have transgressed the commandment of the
> LORD, and thy words: because I feared the people,
> and obeyed their voice. (1 Samuel 15:24)

An individual who was rejected by his natural parents, in particular their father, live a life of trying to gain acceptance of those in authority, yet no matter how much or how good their performance is, the cycle of rejection is something that they just cannot seem to stop. They become obsessively familiar with rejection and try to make adjustments (in the flesh) that will stop the inevitable abortion and destruction of relationships around them. Fear of rejection enters when the individual has done all that they can do but still cannot stop the effects and outcome of rejection. In the back of their mind, they know that something invisible, something from long ago that has been stalking them all their life—it is this something *that* is beyond their control that will show up and deny them, as it has so many times done repeatedly in the past. Then there is self-rejection. Self-rejection comes in when the individual comes to the conclusion that rejection is unavoidable, and it will occur regardless of what they do and so decide to self-destruct the relationships by rejecting themselves before the other individual rejects them. This is a demonic link consisting of rejection, fear of rejection, and self-rejection. These individuals also need deliverance from hurt, deep hurt, and sorrow of heart (Lamentations 3:65). It is important for leaders to get as much deliverance as possible and continue to receive this type of ministry. This will keep the enemy from operating through them in the church. Let me say this to all leaders including myself: we must not become so important and prideful that we cannot receive counsel from others in the body of Christ. Also, we cannot pick and choose who God uses to bring his deliverance. Naaman would have made this mistake and missed his healing had it not been for his servant that helped him see that part of his healing was based on whether or not he could humble himself and obey the instructions of what appeared in his eyes to be a meager servant of the great prophet Elisha. If someone says you need deliverance, take it to heart. It is too risky to ignore. Do not let your pride keep you from receiving the children's bread (Matthew 15:22–28).

How these spirits work

The spirit of rejection will bring in a spirit of control to work with it because this person is afraid that if he or she is not in control of everything, they will not prevail and or be rejected. This person plays into the hand of the enemy by compensating in the flesh what can only be done by the spirit. To compensate means to offset personality weakness. From a psychological perspective, *compensate* is an intransitive verb which means to behave in a way that emphasizes a particular ability or personality trait in order to make up for a deficiency in another. Alfred Adler, founder of the school of individual psychology, introduced the term *compensation* in relation to inferiority feelings. Compensation is a strategy whereby one covers up, consciously or unconsciously, weaknesses frustrations, desires, and feelings of inadequacy or incompetence in one life area through the gratification or (drive toward) excellence in another area. Compensation can cover up either real or imagined deficiencies and personal or physical inferiority. The compensation strategy, however, does not truly address the source of this inferiority.

Identity theft of the kingly anointing[36]

> And David reigned over all Israel; and David executed judgment and justice unto all his people.
> (2 Samuel 8:15)

The problem in many churches is that they don't believe the Lord is a man of war. They still see him as the humble Lamb of God crucified at Calvary. As the Lord starts to rally his church, I believe we are going to see the revelation of the Lord of Hosts because part of the saints' identity has been stolen. Our priestly approach of always praying blessings on those who choose to act as our enemies is completely out of balance. What if God is saying the season is changing and the increase of evil must now be met with the full measure of the King's anointing? If Jesus is ready to judge, our part is demanding justice on the wicked. What if our number one assignment in the last days is praying justice, but the only model we know is praying mercy? Can we overcome our tradition and rise to meet the enemy?[1]

All pastoral training emphasizes Jesus the Savior and has been silent about Jesus the King and Judge. That silence has resulted in an identity theft that now has to be recovered. Will God do it? You can bank on it! Until we can represent Jesus as both Savior and Judge, we are not ready for the level of persecution that confronts the end-time church.[2] We have relegated the Kingly anointing to the marketplace, and many books have been written on that subject.

The truth is the King's anointing is for justice. And it is for wisdom to declare, decree, and to call forth Throne Room justice. It is available for every believer.[3] We represent Jesus as a Priest who forgives sin but do not represent Him as a King who judges and destroys the rebellious.[4] The conflict of earthly kings versus spiritual Kings continues through Psalms 2 Verse 8 describes God's commitment to the conflict that the rulers of the earth incur when they break the bonds and cast away the cords of moral biblical restraint. God is looking for those who will represent Him in declaring, decreeing, prophesying, and calling forth biblical justice.

Verses 8–9 say, "Ask of Me, and I will give You The nations for Your inheritance, And the ends of the earth for Your possession. You shall break them with a rod of iron; You shall dash them in pieces like a potter's vessel."

Verse 12 makes it clear that God is not kidding. He speaks to the political rulers and judges when He says, "Kiss the Son, lest He be angry, And you perish." Perish is the Hebrew word *aw-bad* and it means to be exterminated.

It is the exact same word that David prayed over his own son, Absalom, when Absalom took the throne. Can we hear ministers praying this over rulers and judges today? God said He would do it. Why are we not asking?[5] Can we not recognize that a measure of our spiritual authority has the assignment of representing God as a King in order to draw boundaries against those who practice evil? We've taught the church how to be a Priest. We have failed to teach the church their Kingly responsibility in arresting evil so that it does not defile our harvest field. If the enemy can defile our land before we gain a harvest from it, he guarantees God's judgment on that land and the forfeiture of the harvest. Perhaps that is the enemy's plan. The lack of preparation of the church in this realm is playing into the enemy's hand and must be rectified.[6]

> And from Jesus Christ, who is the faithful witness, and the first begotten of the dead, and the prince of the kings of the earth. Unto him that loved us, and washed us from our sins in his own blood, And hath made us kings and priests unto God and his Father; to him be glory and dominion forever and ever. Amen (Revelation 1:5–6)

Flashback

God is eternal. He is Lord over eternity—past, present, and future. As humans, we experience eternity in a finite way. A common word is flashback. This happens most often in deliverance. The human natural mind and senses of touch, taste, smell, sight, and sound all attached to the soul can trigger what I call eternal past experiences. Because these experiences are activated by the mind and natural senses, what is truth and what is reality in this realm is often influenced by demonic forces (James 3:15). This is why we are instructed to walk by faith. Faith is always in the present or now. The substance of faith (Hebrews 11:1) allows you to access abilities that are mighty through God to the pulling down of strongholds. Faith can never be effectively accessed in the past or the future, because they don't exist. Faith can only be accessed in the present. When a flashback occurs, a person relives eternity past through their mind, which is reflected through their emotions. They feel the way they did during the past experience, and the enemy works hard to convince them that what they feel is truth. If he can, he keeps them in what I call a loop of bondage. Eckhart Tolle (while I do not agree with all of his doctrine) gives a most interesting perspective to this in his book *The Power of Now*.

> Nothing ever happened in the past; it happened in the Now. Nothing ever happen in the future; it will happen in the Now. What you think of as the past is a memory trace, stored in the mind, of a former Now. When you remember the past, you reactivate a memory trace - and you do so now. The future is and imagined Now, a projection of the mind. When the future comes, it comes as the Now when you think about the future, you do it now. Past and future obviously have no reality of their own. Just as the moon has no light of its own, but can only reflect the light of the sun, so are past and future only pale reflections of the light, power and reality of the eternal present. Their reality is borrowed from the Now.[37]

A demon of rage made the following statement to me: "I am there!" As far as I could tell, "there" represents a place along the eternal space-time continuum of the past. This is usually expressed when a person has been emotionally compromised (in deliverance, we call this manifesting) and is flashed back to an eternal past experience that only exists in the mind. Note, it is mentally impossible to be "here" (representing now) and be "there" (representing the past, sometimes referred to as daydreaming) at the same time. Before a person can receive deliverance, they must be brought back to the present or the now. The Bible declares that now is the day of salvation, not the past or the future, but today—at this moment, now.

S.W.A.T. (spiritual weapons and tactics)

Wherefore take unto you the whole armor of God, that ye may be able to withstand in the evil day, and having done all, to stand.

Stand therefore, having your loins girt about with truth, and having on the breastplate of righteousness; And your feet shod with the preparation of the gospel of peace; Above all, taking the shield of faith, wherewith ye shall be able to quench all the fiery darts of the wicked. And take the helmet of salvation, and the sword of the Spirit, which is the word of God. (Ephesians 6:13–17)

These weapons are the actual tools we use to wage war against the enemy, and we arm ourselves with all of God's armor. Let me point out that this armament is not just for apostles but belong to the entire body of Christ, because the body has an apostolic call to the world. Our tools are found in the book Ephesians.

Put on the whole armour of God, that ye may be able to stand against the wiles of the devil. For we wrestle not against flesh and blood, but against principalities, against powers, against the rulers of the darkness of this world, against spiritual wickedness in high places. Wherefore take unto you the whole armour of God, that ye may be able to withstand in the evil day, and having done all, to stand. Stand therefore, having your loins girt about with truth, and having on the breastplate of righteousness; And your feet shod with the preparation of the gospel of peace; Above all, taking the shield of faith, wherewith ye shall be able to quench all the fiery darts of the wicked. And take the helmet of salvation, and the sword of the Spirit, which is the word of God: Praying always with all prayer and supplication in the Spirit, and watching thereunto with all perseverance and supplication for all saints. (Ephesians 6:11–18)

Apostolic people have a pioneering spirit that gives them the grace to go into occupied regions and pull down enemy strongholds. Because of this, those that flow in the apostolic anointing are in a continual confrontation against spiritual forces of darkness that must be dealt with in order to bring deliverance, salvation, and healing. Religion, tradition, and philosophies of men are mindset barriers erected against the truth of God's word and must be demolished. In addition to this, there are certain demonic strongholds (occupied by demons) in the lives of people that cannot be broken until we couple prayer with fasting (Matthew 17:21, Mark 9:29). Prayer and fasting are apostolic tools (weapons) of our warfare. The weapons of our apostolic career are not carnal. These weapons include the name of Jesus, the blood of Jesus, casting out devils, teaching and preaching the gospel of the kingdom, prophesying, fasting and prayer, confession and prayer, laying on of hands, and healing the sick. All these spiritual technologies are accessed by faith; true faith is always in the present tense. Faith is always at this present time. Faith is always now, not past or future.

Apostolic confrontation

Apostles have what I call an in-your-face ministry. They are not afraid to stand toe-to-toe and correct an individual, a faulty doctrine, or mindset in the church.

> But when Peter was come to Antioch, I withstood
> him to the face, because he was to be blamed.
> (Galatians 2:11)

Here Paul takes a stand for righteousness. Apostles are spiritually sensitive with a keen sense of discerning the mind and flow of the Holy Spirit. They also can detect and are sensitive to the operations, plans, and tactics of evil in the spirit realm; and they understand that it only takes a little unrighteousness to overthrow the work of righteousness being worked out by the Spirit within the body of Christ.

> A little leaven leaveneth the whole lump.
> (Galatians 5:9)

Leaven is used as a metaphor of inveterate or incurable mental and moral corruption, viewed in its tendency to infect others. Leaven is applied to that which, though small in quantity yet by its influence, thoroughly pervades a thing.

> Your glorying is not good. Know ye not that a
> little leaven leaveneth the whole lump? Purge
> out therefore the old leaven, that ye may be a
> new lump, as ye are unleavened. For even Christ
> our passover is sacrificed for us: Therefore let us
> keep the feast, not with old leaven, neither with
> the leaven of malice and wickedness; but with
> the unleavened bread of sincerity and truth. (1
> Corinthians 5:6–8)

Apostles confront the leaven in the lives of others not to condemn but to purge, recover, and restore those that have been affected and lead away, knowing that a little leaven will spoil the holiness of the work and lead others to stumble or fall away from the truth.

> For before that certain came from James, he did
> eat with the Gentiles: but when they were come,
> he withdrew and separated himself, fearing them
> which were of the circumcision. And the other
> Jews dissembled likewise with him; insomuch
> that Barnabas also was carried away with their
> dissimulation. (Galatians 2:12–13)

Apostles are driven and consumed with establishing the righteousness of God.

> But when I saw that they walked not uprightly
> according to the truth of the gospel, I said unto
> Peter before them all, If thou, being a Jew, livest
> after the manner of Gentiles, and not as do the
> Jews, why compellest thou the Gentiles to live as
> do the Jews? (Galatians 2:14)

The apostle's probing character and unquenchable thirst and zeal for righteousness often times stir up or uncover things that others would rather they left alone. As previously stated, apostles have been graced by God to inspect, test, and challenge. Depending on the scope of the "rule," apostolic grace will confront false doctrine, theology, and mindsets in individuals in the local and corporate church, locally, nationally, and internationally, and as we get closer to the return of Jesus, I believe this grace will have a global effect on the church.

> But we will not boast of things without our measure, but according to the measure of the rule which God hath distributed to us, a measure to reach even unto you. (2 Corinthians 10:13)

In the above scripture, the word *rule* comes from the word *kanon*, which means a definitely bound or fixed space within the limits of which one's power of influence is confined, the province assigned one's sphere of activity. Apostolic prophetic preaching and teaching confronts darkness, demolishing falsehoods and mental strongholds, and strongholds in the heavens and upon the waters.

> See, I have this day set thee over the nations and over the kingdoms, to root out, and to pull down, and to destroy, and to throw down, to build, and to plant. (Jeremiah 1:10)

> Then, as a wise masterbuilder, lays the only foundation that has eternal significance, which is Christ. (1 Corinthians 3:10–11)

Confrontation is a characteristic of the spiritually violent.

> And from the days of John the Baptist until now the kingdom of heaven suffereth violence, and the violent take it by force. (Matthew 11:12)

We are to engage the enemy.

> Rise ye up, take your journey, and pass over the
> river Arnon: behold, I have given into thine hand
> Sihon the Amorite, king of Heshbon, and his
> land: begin to possess it, and contend with him
> in battle. This day will I begin to put the dread of
> thee and the fear of thee upon the nations that are
> under the whole heaven, who shall hear report of
> thee, and shall tremble, and be in anguish because
> of thee. (Deuteronomy 2:24–25)

These saints are in such hot pursuit of the lover of their souls that obstacles, strongholds, demons, even the gates of hell, are only barriers to be broken. Fasting and prayer makes confrontation with the forces of darkness unavoidable. The only way to walk in freedom from that which restrains you is to confront it. Some people never confronted their belly until they started fasting. They never realized how much influence their stomach has over them until they go on a fast. Sad to say, some people come to the realization that their stomach is their god. They simply cannot overcome their fleshly desire. This is your first battle, but who will win? The real you, the new man (Ephesians 4:24), or the old man, lustful and corrupt (Ephesians 4:22), motivated and controlled by fleshly appetites? Some saints have called a truce with their adversary simply because they are afraid to confront him. This is the first battle that you must win. It is a battle that Jesus wants you to win, because if you do not win this battle, you cannot be his disciple. Born again? Yes. Water-baptized? Yes. Spirit-filled? Yes. Speaking in tongues? Yes. Going to heaven? Yes. Disciple? No.

> And he said to them all, if any man will come
> after me, let him deny himself, and take up his
> cross daily, and follow me. (Luke 9:23)

The "self-life" is the one of the most wicked things imaginable. It should not be trusted. It is deceptive; it lies, justifies sin and, believe me, it does not want to die. But you must kill it! God does not use living people; he only uses dead, resurrected people in the church to accomplish his will, plan, and purpose. You must die to self. Fasting puts "self" on your own personal cross so it can get what it deserves—DEATH!

> And whosoever doth not bear his cross, and come
> after me, cannot be my disciple. (Luke 14:27)

> I am crucified with Christ: nevertheless I live; yet
> not I, but Christ liveth in me: and the life which I
> now live in the flesh I live by the faith of the Son
> of God, who loved me, and gave himself for me.
> (Galatians 2:20)

Here's a revelation for all you profoundly deep folks: "Until you confront certain things in your life, they will never change." A sister shared with our fellowship how bound she was before joining our church; she said she was so depressed that when she got home, she would go to her room and literally pull the blankets up over her head. She simply did not want to face or confront anything in her life. Thank God that today she is delivered.

The Lord wants us to confront the things we avoid. When we do not confront issues, we will walk, talk, even pray around them, avoiding and pretending that they do not exist. Sooner or later, we have to confront them because they're vexing us. They are pulling us down, making us miserable, angry, and upset, and most likely blocking our blessing. But we just don't want to deal with these issues, and subconsciously, we wish they would just go away, but they won't. We must confront them!

Apostolic interface

An "interface" is a kind of convergence, intersection, an overlap. It is a representation of common ground between theories or phenomena. An interface in computer science is a computer circuit consisting of the hardware and associated circuitry that links one device with another—a hard disk drive, printer, monitor, or other peripheral. The interface gives each component the ability to connect with the main CPU (computer processing unit) to function in unison as one.

Traditionally, our churches have been built around the pastor as set man. This model of building is found nowhere in Scripture and in most cases become a one-man show. The New Testament prototype (Antioch church) is built upon plurality of leadership within the local church. The pastoral anointing lacks the grace and capacity to interface with governmental gifts (apostles, prophets, and teachers) in such a way as to set them in the functional apostolic order of the New Testament church. Only the gift of the apostle can do that. However, prophets and those with prophetic giftings can recognize true apostolic grace (see John 1:29, John 1:36, and Luke 2:25–38). Apostles have been gifted and anointed by God to interface with other ministry gifts in the body of Christ. The apostles' anointing brings order, unity, and oneness. Apostles are team players. They have a unique ability to see the gifts and callings on the lives of others and direct them into their destiny. Although it is not exclusive, below I have listed some of the many ways that apostles interface with the gifts in the body of Christ.

1. Apostles recognize ministry gifts

> When I call to remembrance the unfeigned faith that is in thee, which dwelt first in thy grandmother Lois, and thy mother Eunice; and I am persuaded that in thee also. (2 Timothy 1:5)

> Neglect not the gift that is in thee, which was given thee by prophecy, with the laying on of the hands of the presbytery. (1 Timothy 4:14)

2. Apostles activate and impart into ministry gifts

> Wherefore I put thee in remembrance that thou stir up the gift of God, which is in thee by the putting on of my hands. (2 Timothy 1:6)

3. Apostles proclaim doctrine and establish the faith

> And as they went (Paul and Timotheus), through the cities, they delivered them the decrees for to keep, that were ordained of the apostles and elders which were at Jerusalem. And so were the churches established in the faith, and increased in number daily. (Acts 16:4-5)

4. Apostles set ministry gifts in order

> And when they had ordained them elders in every church, and had prayed with fasting, they commended them to the Lord, on whom they believed Acts 14:23.

> As they ministered to the Lord, and fasted, the Holy Ghost said, Separate me Barnabas and Saul for the work whereunto I have called them. And when they had fasted and prayed, and laid their hands on them, they sent them away. (Acts 13:2)

5. Apostles acknowledge, embrace, and celebrate ministry gifts

> Greet Priscilla and Aquila my helpers in Christ Jesus: Who have for my life laid down their own necks: unto whom not only I give thanks, but also all the churches of the Gentiles. Likewise greet the church that is in their house. Salute my wellbeloved Epaenetus, who is the first fruits of

Achaia unto Christ. Greet Mary, who bestowed much labour on us. Salute Andronicus and Junia, my kinsmen, and my fellowprisoners, who are of note among the apostles, who also were in Christ before me. Greet Amplias my beloved in the Lord. Salute Urbane, our helper in Christ, and Stachys my beloved. Salute Apelles approved in Christ. Salute them which are of Aristobulus' household. Salute Herodion my kinsman. Greet them that be of the household of Narcissus, which are in the Lord. Salute Tryphena and Tryphosa, who labour in the Lord. Salute the beloved Persis, which laboured much in the Lord. Salute Rufus chosen in the Lord, and his mother and mine. Salute Asyncritus, Phlegon, Hermas, Patrobas, Hermes, and the brethren which are with them. Salute Philologus, and Julia, Nereus, and his sister, and Olympas, and all the saints which are with them. (Romans 16:3–15)

6. Apostles adjust correct and set the church in order

And if any man hunger, let him eat at home; that ye come not together unto condemnation. And the rest will I set in order when I come. (1 Corinthians 11:34)

7. Apostles organize and mobilize ministry gifts in the church

Then pleased it the apostles and elders with the whole church, to send chosen men of their own company to Antioch with Paul and Barnabas; namely, Judas surnamed Barsabas and Silas, chief men among the brethren. (Acts 15:22)

But ye know the proof of him, that, as a son with the father, he hath served with me in the gospel. Him therefore I hope to send presently, so soon as I shall see how it will go with me. But I trust in the Lord that I also myself shall come shortly. Yet I supposed it necessary to send to you Epaphroditus, my brother, and companion in labour, and fellowsoldier, but your messenger, and he that ministered to my wants. (Philippians 2:22–25)

8

Fasting

From a biblical perspective, fasting is more than just not eating. "Religious fasting is a duty required of the Disciples of Christ, but it is not so much a duty itself, as it is a means to dispose us for other duties. Fasting is the humbling of the soul" (Matthew Henry).

Even with this definition, we must be careful in our understanding of the origins of fasting. Fasting is not something that man has devised (through the guise of religion) to attain piety; on the contrary, fasting was instituted by God in the Old Testament economy. Under Mosaic law God's people were instructed to fast once annually. It was called the "Day of Atonement." It expressed their need of cleansing and forgiveness.

> And this shall be a statute forever unto you: that in the seventh month, on the tenth day of the month, ye shall afflict your souls, and do no work at all, whether it be one of your own country, or a stranger that sojourneth among you: For on that day shall the priest make an atonement for you, to cleanse you, that ye may be clean from all your sins before the LORD. (Leviticus 16:29–30)

This statute in the book of Leviticus established a corporate national day of fasting to annually atone for the nation of Israel's sin.

Although individual fasting is not commanded, it is strongly implied (Matthew 6:16); and voluntary fasting appears frequently under the old economy as well as the New Testament experience.

Four technologies of fasting

Although there are many ways in which one may fast, all fasts can be categorized into four basic types:

Partial. The partial fast is found twice in the book of Daniel. In the first instance, Daniel abstained from eating the royal cuisine. Second, he abstained from flesh, wine and what is referred to as pleasant bread.

> But Daniel purposed in his heart that he would not defile himself with the portion of the king's meat, nor with the wine which he drank: therefore he requested of the prince of the eunuchs that he might not defile himself. (Daniel 1:8)

> Prove thy servants, I beseech thee, ten days; and let them give us pulse to eat, and water to drink. (Daniel 1:12)

Daniel ate "pulse," a kind of vegetable, and drank water for three years. On his next partial fast, he excluded particular foods and ate no pleasant bread.

> In those days I Daniel was mourning three full weeks. I ate no pleasant bread, neither came flesh nor wine in my mouth. (Daniel 10:2–3)

Absolute. The absolute fast allows neither food nor liquids. Under normal conditions, individuals do not start fasting at the absolute level; however, extreme circumstances seem to prompt or thrust an individual into this type of fast. It was not under normal conditions in which Saul (also known as Paul) came to know the Lord. While on this way to Damascus, he was knocked to the ground and blinded; after which he fasted for three days. This is the absolute fast.

> And Saul arose from the earth; and when his eyes
> were opened, he saw no man: but they led him by
> the hand, and brought him into Damascus. And
> he was three days without sight, and neither did
> eat nor drink. (Acts 9:8–9)

So far, we have looked at two of the four types of fasts found in the Bible, the partial and the absolute. Next, I want to look at perhaps the most functionally powerful of the all the types—the corporate absolute fast.

Corporate absolute. Haman, an agent of Satan, is used to plot the destruction of God's people, the Jews. In the book of Esther, a decree of death to all Jews is sealed by the king's ring. It is important to note that this decree is immutable; it cannot be altered. Facing certain extinction, the Jews called a fast-seeking intervention from the hand of God to prevent a holocaust.

> Go, gather together all the Jews that are present
> in Shushan, and fast ye for me, and neither eat
> nor drink three days, night or day: I also and my
> maidens will fast likewise; and so will I go in unto
> the king, which is not according to the law: and if
> I perish, I perish. (Esther 4:16)

After Mordecai charged Esther (Esther 4:8) that she should go to the king and make supplication for her people, notice in the above verse that Esther instructs all the Jews in Shushan to fast for "her." The reasoning for this was twofold: number one, it was unlawful to approach the king's throne unless summoned, and violators were punishable by death unless the king held out his golden scepter, allowing one to approach. Consequently, Esther first needed God to extend mercy to her through King Ahasuerus. God's mercy is obvious by the king's kindness. Supplication in the Hebrew language is the word Chanan which means—to bend or stoop in kindness to an inferior; to favor, bestow, causative to implore (that is to move to favor by petition). God's response to our sincere supplication is with mercy and grace.

> Then said the king unto her, What wilt thou, queen Esther? And what is thy request? It shall be even given thee to the half of the kingdom. (Esther 5:3)

Number two; this is a time of great need for the Jewish people. Esther purposed within herself that she would be God's instrument of grace laying down her life for the lives of her people. The mercy that the Jews need can only be obtained by approaching king Ahasuerus's throne; mercy is a powerful force. Today, because of the rich, righteous, redeeming blood of Jesus and his completed work on the cross, we can come boldly to the "throne of grace" to obtain mercy and find grace to help in our time of need (Hebrews 4:16).

The power of mercy

There is only one force in the world that can stand toe-to-toe and face-to-face with the judgment of God and prevail. This is the power of "mercy." I will never forget the lesson I learned and the supernatural manifestation of mercy that I witnessed while living in Illinois. I needed to pick up a computer peripheral at a store in downtown Chicago. I clearly saw the no parking sign that said No parking, No standing, No loading. However, I thought to myself that because I had preordered the product and the people in the store would have it at the counter waiting for me, it would be all right to leave my car in this no-parking zone. I knew it would take less than two minutes to make the transaction because I had a purchase order. So I left my car in the no-parking zone, went into the store, and was out in less than two minutes. When I walked out the door of the store, I saw my car being raised in the air by a Chicago tow truck. The first words out of my mouth were, "Oh God they are towing my car!" and the Lord said, "You saw the sign." That is not what I wanted to hear; nevertheless, when the Lord said that, I realized that I was under judgment for willfully disobeying the no parking sign. I went to the tow truck driver lifting my car and told him that I would move it and that there was no reason to tow it. He acted as though he did not hear me. I said, "If you tow my car like that, you will damage the front suspension," and he said "No, I have this model myself; it will be fine."

So I said to him, "How much is my fine for parking here?"

He said, "It will cost you two hundred dollars to get your car out of the city pound."

Pound! I said, "Oh no, let me pay you here; I don't want the car to go to the pound." (I knew all sorts of damage could occur at the pound.) I offered to pay the ticket in advance of the pound, but he would not take it. I had check, cash, and credit card, and he would not take any of it. Once I determined that he was going to tow my car and that there was nothing I could do to stop him, I told him that I was going to sit in the car while he towed it so I could be sure no damage or vandalism occurred at the pound. He walked over to my car, opened the door, and said, "Sir, please get out of the car or I will be forced to call the police." I got out of the car, and as the tow truck driver walked back toward his truck, I knew that I had tried everything I could think of to keep my car from being towed; so I prayed, "Lord, please help me!"

The Lord said, "Ask him to forgive you." It sounded very strange to me, but I knew it was a clear word from the Lord; and besides, I had run out of options.

I walked over to the man and said, "Sir, would you please forgive me for parking my car here?" He then looked at me very strange, his whole demeanor changed, and he got out of his truck, walked to the back of truck, and started lowering my car to the ground. (I could hardly believe it.) And all the while he's doing this, he's talking out loud saying, "I did not know that this was *your* car… How was I supposed to know that this was *your* car. I am a tow truck driver. I tow cars—that's what I do. How was I supposed to know this was *your* car." And, to my surprise, all the while he is talking, he is unhooking my car from his tow truck. When he finished, I wanted to thank him and shake his hand, but he would not let me, pointing out that people were looking and that they would say that I gave him money. So I asked him what he had need of, and I told him that I was going to ask God to bless him for being a blessing to me. He told me, and a moment afterward started repeating what he had been saying before. "I did not know this was *your* car. How was I supposed to know that this was *your* car?" It was as if he was talking to another person or that he was viewing me as another person. I could not tell. It is hard to explain, but I know something supernatural happened and caused this man to suddenly change his mind completely about towing my car; and it did not happen until I acted on the word that God gave me.

I believe I witnessed a manifestation of mercy. I could have mistaken this for something else if I had not been in the situation I was in prior to mercy showing up. Many times in the Bible when mercy is mentioned, it is in the context of mercy being shown, someone showing someone else mercy, or God showing mercy. Mercy can be seen! I have seen it! Not only did God deliver me out of that situation; he did it by showing me mercy (literally). He also allowed me to see in an instant the force of mercy meeting judgment; and on top of it all, he gave me favor with the tow truck driver. As I said previously, mercy is the only force that can prevail against God's judgment, or any other judgment, for that matter. When mercy shows up, judgment must back down.

> But the LORD was with Joseph, and shewed him
> mercy, and gave him favour in the sight of the
> keeper of the prison. (Genesis 39:21)

"Showed him mercy" are words that do my heart well. Keep in mind that mercy seems to always show up (or someone shows mercy) during or after some sort of pending judgment. Let us look at what happened prior to the Lord showing Joseph mercy.

> And it came to pass, when his master heard the words of his wife, which she spake unto him, saying, After this manner did thy servant [Joseph] to me; that his wrath was kindled. And Joseph's master took him, and put him into the prison, a place where the king's prisoners were bound: and he was there in the prison. (Genesis 39:19–20)

But the LORD shewed him mercy "Hallelujah!" Of course Joseph did not deserve that prison sentence, but showing him mercy was a part of God's divine plan for his life. Mercy can also be released through fasting. Let's take a look at group of people who accessed mercy through a corporate absolute fast.

> Now the word of the LORD came unto Jonah the son of Amittai, saying, Arise, go to Nineveh, that great city, and cry against it; for their wickedness is come up before me. (Jonah 1:1–2)

It seems that the wickedness of Nineveh had reached the proportions of Sodom and Gomorrah. The city had become so evil that God had to send a prophet crying in the streets warning the city of imminent judgment and destruction. Jonah walked the streets and cried, saying, "In forty days this city will be destroyed; in forty days Nineveh will be overthrown." Everyone in the city heard his message, and what happens next is amazing.

> So the people of Nineveh believed God, and proclaimed a fast, and put on sackcloth, from the greatest of them even to the least of them. For word came unto the king of Nineveh, and he

arose from his throne, and he laid his robe from
him, and covered him with sackcloth, and sat
in ashes. And he caused it to be proclaimed and
published through Nineveh by the decree of the
king and his nobles, saying, let neither man nor
beast, herd nor flock, taste any thing: let them
not feed, nor drink water. But let man and beast
be covered with sackcloth, and cry mightily unto
God: yea, let them turn everyone from his evil
way, and from the violence that is in their hands.
(Jonah 3:5–8)

Every man, woman, boy, and child was included, from the
hobo on the street to the king's palace; everybody fasted. Even the
family beasts (dogs, cats, and goldfish), herds, or flocks according to
the kings' decree could not eat or drink. Also, in the kings' decree:

Let man and beast be covered with sackcloth, and
cry mightily unto God. (Jonah 3:8)

Can you envision what this city must have looked like with
everyone including the cows, horses, flocks, cats, and dogs all wear-
ing sackcloth? It must have been a sight to see. These people were
serious; they knew they had the sentence of death and became des-
perate before God. It was either a corporate absolute fast or literal
death and annihilation. Their only hope was the mercy of God.

And God saw their works, that they turned from
their evil way; and God repented of the evil, that
he had said that he would do unto them; and he
did it not. (Jonah 3:10)

This corporate fast moved the heart of God. The judgment of
God's fierce anger against Nineveh was changed to his tender mercies
in one day because they fasted corporately. There seems to be a grace
released similar to that of the anointing. An individual anointing is

powerful; however, when believers combine their anointing, coming together in unity with one mind and one purpose, a powerful, unstoppable force is released (the corporate anointing), and something greater than multiplication (a quantum leap) takes place.

> And five of you shall chase an hundred, and an hundred of you shall put ten thousand to flight: and your enemies shall fall before you by the sword. (Leviticus 26:8)

> How should one chase a thousand, and two put ten thousand to flight, except their Rock had sold them, and the LORD had shut them up? (Deuteronomy 32:30)

The corporate anointing is the most powerful anointing there is. Likewise, with fasting, there is power when we fast alone, but much greater power when the church fasts corporately. When the whole body of Christ comes together to fast and pray, supernatural, apostolic global evangelism will erupt, with power to transform the nations, releasing deliverance to heal the brokenhearted, to preach deliverance to the captives, recover sight to the blind, and to set at liberty them that are bruised. We will witness the love and mercies of God, break through, and proclaiming his kingdom in places where the gospel has never been preached and establishing the foundation of the gospel of Christ in places it has never been laid.

The technology of unity and oneness

> I therefore, the prisoner of the Lord, beseech you that ye walk worthy of the vocation wherewith ye are called, With all lowliness and meekness, with longsuffering, forbearing one another in love; Endeavouring to keep the unity of the Spirit in the bond of peace. (Ephesians 4:1–3)

Something supernatural takes place even when the unsaved come into agreement and together become one.

> And the whole earth was of one language, and of one speech. And it came to pass, as they journeyed from the east, that they found a plain in the land of Shinar; and they dwelt there. And they said one to another, Go to, let us make brick, and burn them thoroughly. And they had brick for stone, and slime had they for morter. And they said, Go to, let us build us a city and a tower, whose top may reach unto heaven; and let us make us a name, lest we be scattered abroad upon the face of the whole earth. And the LORD came down to see the city and the tower, which the children of men builded. And the LORD said, Behold, the people is one, and they have all one language; and this they begin to do: and now nothing will be restrained from them, which they have imagined to do. (Genesis 11:1–6)

Notice it says, "now nothing will be restrained from them, which they have imagined to do." This became possible when this group of heathens tapped into the technology of oneness. God had to go down and confuse the language of the people to stop them from literally building a gateway from earth to heaven. This is the power of oneness that previously existed in the natural realm before God overthrew it. However, there is a spiritual dimension of this same power available to the people of God.

> And when the day of Pentecost was fully come, they were all with one accord in one place. And suddenly there came a sound from heaven as of a rushing mighty wind, and it filled all the house where they were sitting. And there appeared unto them cloven tongues like as of fire, and it sat

upon each of them. And they were all filled with
the Holy Ghost, and began to speak with other
tongues, as the Spirit gave them utterance. (Acts
2:1–4)

Whereas God confused the language at the Tower of Babel in
his earlier dealings with mankind, he then pours out his Spirit and
ignites the birthing of the church with the fiery native language of the
nation of heaven on the day of Pentecost. The body of Christ has one
Lord, one faith, and are born again by one baptism (1 Corinthians
12:13, Ephesians 4:5); and through the outpouring of the baptism in
the Holy Spirt all share a common tongue. The Lord uses prayer to
bring his body into unison with his plan, purpose, and move of his
Spirit. Oneness among God's people can be accessed through prayer
(Acts 4:23–31). Oneness is a powerful technology of the Spirit that
releases the supernatural (see Acts 12:5–17).

I believe the Lord will use this principal of oneness to mobilize
the body of Christ simultaneously around the world in the coming days to do the work of the ministry. The gospel of the kingdom
will be preached worldwide, accomplishing his endgame (Matthew
24:14) on a grand scale. This will usher in the greater works (John
14:12) of corporate Christ moving in oneness and unity of the Spirit.
No matter how great the denominational divide looks today, the true
body of Christ will become one because this is what Jesus prayed.

Neither pray I for these alone, but for them also
which shall believe on me through their word;
That they all may be one; as thou, Father, art in
me, and I in thee, that they also may be one in
us: that the world may believe that thou hast sent
me. And the glory which thou gavest me I have
given them; that they may be one, even as we
are one: I in them, and thou in me, that they
may be made perfect in one; and that the world
may know that thou hast sent me, and hast loved
them, as thou hast loved me. (John 17:20–23)

As we saw at the Tower of Babel when the people became one, they potentially become unstoppable. They possessed the power to literally do what is literally impossible. Unity, on the other hand, is much different; people can decide to unite around a common purpose yet having different agendas, still not reaching the quantum state of oneness.

Two thousand years ago, 120 believers all gathered together with one accord in one place, waiting and believing to receive the promise of the Father (Luke 24:49, Acts 1:4–5, Acts 1:8). As a result, God poured out his Spirit, birth the church, and sparked a revival whose fires still burn today. Individually, one prays for the blessings of God—asking, seeking, and knocking (Matthew 7:7–8)—but corporately, where there is unity of the Spirit, God commands the blessing.

> Behold, how good and how pleasant it is for brethren to dwell together in unity! It is like the precious ointment upon the head, that ran down upon the beard, even Aaron's beard: that went down to the skirts of his garments; As the dew of Hermon, and as the dew that descended upon the mountains of Zion: for there the LORD commanded the blessing, even life for evermore. (Psalm 133:1–3)

In the book of Jonah, we have seen a clear picture of this unity and oneness algorithm and the yield release of tremendous power through the corporate absolute fast. The use of the superlative "tremendous power" is relative to the fact that this fast was initiated by people that were not in covenant with God; nevertheless, they were able to stay God's hand from judgment and destruction on the city Nineveh by applying the technology of fasting. If God can be moved in this fashion by the humbled heathen, how much more abundantly will he respond to a remnant of his children who have the promise of this technology (2 Chronicles 7:14) and are called by his name? This illustration reveals not just the power of this type of fast, but also the inconceivable capacity of this technology to influence the heart and hand of God. This is the power of the corporate absolute fast.

Supernatural absolute fast

While the scriptures record Jesus and Elijah both fasting forty days and nights, Moses is the only person that the Bible clearly shows fasted for forty days and forty nights without food or water, which by all scientific standards is humanly impossible. But what's even more astonishing is the fact that Moses did this twice.

> And the Lord said unto Moses, Write thou these words: for after the tenor of these words I have made a covenant with thee and with Israel. And he was there with the LORD forty days and forty nights; he did neither eat bread, nor drink water. And he wrote upon the tables the words of the covenant, the Ten Commandments. (Exodus 34:27–28)

> And I fell down before the Lord, as at the first, forty days and forty nights: I did neither eat bread, nor drink water, because of all your sins which ye sinned, in doing wickedly in the sight of the Lord, to provoke him to anger. (Deuteronomy 9:18)

Although the body can survive significantly longer without food, there must be some sort of divine technological engagement to survive this type of extended fast devoid of food and water.

I call this the *Supernatural Absolute Fast* because in our natural physical state, it is impossible for our body to survive forty days without water, but with God, all things are possible (Matthew 19:26b). Fasting of this sort can only be characterized as someone living in another dimension, thereby enabling them to circumvent the natural laws of the physical body.

The Glory Realm

Earlier in this segment, I said that fasting of this sort can only be characterized as someone living in another dimension. I call this dimension "The Glory Realm." This dimension is a place or locality near God that encompasses all his goodness. I believe that the glory realm is a dimension near God where time and eternity converge or overlap and the law of physics is suspended.

A place by me

The book of Exodus records a very intimate and revealing conversation between Moses and God. In this conversation, the scripture gives us insight into the existence and reality of this dimensional plain of God's presence that God calls a place by me. Without the following scriptural reference, conceivably, we could, in no way, have discerned or discovered the reality of this truth on our own.

> And he said, My presence shall go with thee, and I will give thee rest. And he said unto him, If thy presence go not with me, carry us not up hence. For wherein shall it be known here that I and thy people have found grace in thy sight? is it not in that thou goest with us? so shall we be separated, I and thy people, from all the people that are upon the face of the earth.
>
> And the LORD said unto Moses, I will do this thing also that thou hast spoken: for thou hast found grace in my sight, and I know thee by name.

And he said, I beseech thee, shew me thy glory. And he said, I will make all my goodness pass before thee, and I will proclaim the name of the LORD before thee; and will be gracious to whom I will be gracious, and will shew mercy on whom I will shew mercy.

And he said, Thou canst not see my face: for there shall no man see me, and live. And the LORD said, Behold, there is a place by me, and thou shalt stand upon a rock:

And it shall come to pass, while my glory passeth by, that I will put thee in a clift of the rock, and will cover thee with my hand while I pass by: And I will take away mine hand, and thou shalt see my back parts: but my face shall not be seen. (Exodus 33: 14–23)

In the above scripture, Moses asked God for his tangible presence to accompany him and the people on their journey from Egypt. God's displayed presence is witnessed in the Old Testament as a cloud by day and a pillar of fire by night in Exodus 13:21–22, Exodus 40:38, Numbers 14:14, and Deuteronomy 1:33.

Notice also in this scripture, when Moses asked to see God's glory, God responded by saying: "No man can see my face and live." Here, we establish the fact that the face of God is the glory of God. Yet, what may seem contradictive is what God said about Moses in the book of Numbers.

I speak with him face to face, even plainly, and not in dark sayings; and he sees the form of the LORD. (Numbers 12:8 NKJV)

I would like to submit to you that even though Moses talked to God face-to-face and saw the form of the Lord, he was still talking and looking through a cloud that shrouded the Lord's appearance. This is why Moses begged God to see his face; he wanted to see the

Lord plainly without the cloud covering. I believe the Lord was protecting Moses because looking directly into the face of the living God would be nothing short of spontaneous combustion; the scripture says that God is a consuming fire (Hebrews 12:29). Now, let's look at God's alternative solution to what Moses requested.

In Exodus 33:21, the Lord says, "Behold, there is a place by me." This place by God is what I call the Glory Realm or Realm of Glory. It is the *holy* space or *holy* atmosphere surrounding God's throne. It is the closest proximity to God that an individual or group of individuals can be in without being physically consumed by the glory of God's magnificent brilliance. Examples of the glory realm are found in Isaiah 6:1–7 and Revelations 4:8.

When a person or group of people enter the glory realm, this divine atmosphere of goodness, the natural laws of physics, are evaded in the glory realm; physical laws no longer apply. God tells Moses that he will put him in a fissure of the rock, cover him with his hand, and make all his goodness pass before him, then he takes away his hand so Mosses can see his back parts, but not God's face. In this place by God, all that is good about God is on display, though his face is not revealed. The effects of the glory realm can be seen throughout the Bible. In Exodus 3:2–3, "a bush that burned with fire, and yet the bush was not consumed."

> Clothing and shoes that do not wear out. (Deuteronomy 29:5)

> Aaron's rod that brought forth buds, bloomed blossoms, and yielded almonds. (Numbers 17:7–8)

> Handkerchiefs and aprons bring healing and deliverance. (Acts 19:11–12)

> Five loaves plus two fish feed five thousand men and seven loaves and a few little fish feeds four

thousand men plus the women and children. (Mark 6:41–44, Mathew 15:36–38)

An iron axe head swims. (2 Kings 6:5–7)

While there are many more examples that we could mention, perhaps the most vivid spectacular and miraculous demonstration of the glory realm is found in Daniel chapter 3.

> And these three men, Shadrach, Meshach, and Abednego, fell down bound into the midst of the burning fiery furnace.
> Then Nebuchadnezzar the king was astonied, and rose up in haste, and spake, and said unto his counsellors, Did not we cast three men bound into the midst of the fire? They answered and said unto the king, True, O king. He answered and said, Lo, I see four men loose, walking in the midst of the fire, and they have no hurt; and the form of the fourth is like the Son of God.
> Then Nebuchadnezzar came near to the mouth of the burning fiery furnace, and spake, and said, Shadrach, Meshach, and Abednego, ye servants of the most high God, come forth, and come hither. Then Shadrach, Meshach, and Abednego, came forth of the midst of the fire.
> And the princes, governors, and captains, and the king's counsellors, being gathered together, saw these men, upon whose bodies the fire had no power, nor was an hair of their head singed, neither were their coats changed, nor the smell of fire had passed on them. (Daniel 3:23–27)

Your desire, your want, your will

> And thou shalt love the LORD thy God with all
> thine heart, and with all thy soul, and with all thy
> might. (Deuteronomy 6:5)

Let me be very candid here. For the most part, people do what they want to do. When we were in the world without Christ, we did what we wanted to do no matter how difficult, exasperating, or far-fetched it seemed. When we lived in sin, we were faithful to serve our sin master well and willingly. On the weekends, some of us could not wait to get to the nightclub to spend a weeks' salary worshiping the deception called "a good time," which sometimes resulted in waking up the next morning wondering what happened!

Now, we have made a decision to serve the living God. Because he freed us from our bondage to sin, we now have the will to choose right or wrong, good or evil. He will not tamper with our will nor will he make choices for us (Deuteronomy 30:19). Having a will makes you and I free moral agents to make choices; be they right or wrong, God has given us all the right to choose. However, we must understand that what we desire or want is connected to a reward. We do what we want to do because we want the reward that fulfills our desire; therefore, a reward has potential influence over our will.

When looking back at the initial sin in the garden, we come to understand that what Eve wanted or desired corresponded with a reward (Genesis 3:4–6). This shows that the reward she desired and had affections for influenced her will against God's will and commandment (1 John 2:16–17). The enemy knows that if he can control your "will," he can control you and manipulate your destiny. Since he could not stop you from making a decision for Christ as Lord of your life, his next plan is to render you ineffective in God's kingdom by seeking to control your will through your desires. Your will can be influenced by what you want or desire emotionally. This is why scripture instructs us to set our affection on things above, not on things on the earth (Colossians 3:2). The enemy entices with a reward to generate a desire as he did in the garden, and if left unchecked, a desire in the heart becomes the pursuit of the will.

The key in overcoming this trap, as Watchman Nee points out in his book, *The Spiritual Man*, is to love the Lord with all of our heart. Nee reveals the linkage of the mind, the will, and the emotions and points out how the enemy used these areas to cause the fall of man and how he continues today using the same method, causing individuals to sin, therefore bringing them into bondage. The most important parts of man's soul are his mind, will, and emotion. The will is the master of man; it is the organ of deliberation. The mind is the thinking organ while the emotion is the loving organ.

The apostle told us that "Adam was not deceived" (1 Timothy 2:14). This shows that Adam's mind was not confused. The one who was weak in mind and intellect was Eve. "But the woman, having been quite deceived, has fallen into transgression" (1 Timothy 2:14). The record of Genesis says, "The woman said, The serpent beguiled me, and I did eat" (3:13). Adam said, "The woman whom thou gavest to be with me, she gave [not beguiled] me of the tree, and I did eat" (v. 12). Adam was not beguiled; his mind was still clear. He knew that the fruit was the forbidden fruit. Yet he ate it because of his emotion. Adam knew that all the words of the serpent were the deceptions of the enemy. When we read the word of the apostle, we find that Adam sinned purposely and was not like Eve who sinned through being beguiled. He loved Eve more than himself. He idolized her and loved her so much that he rebelled against the commandment of the Lord for her sake. How pitiful this was. His head was controlled by his heart, and his reason was overcome by his love. Why have men "not believed the truth"? It is because they "have taken pleasure in unrighteousness" (2 Thessalonians 2:12). It is not because reason is lacking, but because the desire is lacking. Therefore, when a man truly turns to the Lord "with the heart [and not with the head,] there is believing unto righteousness" (Romans 10:10). Satan gained Adam's will through his emotion, and caused him to sin. The way Satan beguiled Eve was to confuse her mind, gain her will, and then cause her to sin. When man's will, mind, and emotion were poisoned by the serpent to follow Satan and to rebel against God, the spirit with which man communicates with God received a fatal blow. Here we see the principle of Satan's work. He beguiled man's soul to sin through the things of the flesh (the eating of the fruit). Once the soul has sinned, the spirit falls into darkness and degradation. This is the order of all his works—from the outside to the inside. Either he works from man's body, or he works from his mind or his emotion for the purpose of gaining his will. Once man's will surrenders, Satan gains the whole being, and the spirit is put to death. The way he worked the first time is the way he works in all subsequent times. God's work is always from the inside to the outside. He first works from man's spirit, then enlightens man's mind, touches man's emotion, and finally causes man to exercise his will to activate his body to carry out God's will. All the devil's works go from the outside to the inside, while all the works of God's Spirit go from the inside to the outside. In this way, we can differentiate what is of God and what is of Satan. This shows us that once Satan gains man's will, he controls man.[38]

> But every man is tempted, when he is drawn
> away of his own lust, and enticed. Then when
> lust hath conceived, it bringeth forth sin: and sin,
> when it is finished, bringeth forth death. (James
> 1:14–15)

So who is in control of your "will," your spirit man or your belly? This is personal warfare (taking up your cross), a fight that you must win, because greater battles can never be won until you crucify the flesh; and fasting is the way to do it. This matter is so fundamental that Jesus said that without it, you cannot be his disciple ("disciplined one"). It is so crucial that the Bible says you should cut your throat if you cannot control your eating.

> And put a knife to thy throat, if thou be a man
> given to appetite. (Proverbs 23:2)

Hold up! I don't want you to hurt yourself. The simple truth is that some people are just in love with food. Fasting can help break the power of the flesh so you can adjust your will and reset your affections.

> Set your affection on things above, not on things
> on the earth. (Colossians 3:2)

> This I say then, Walk in the Spirit, and ye shall
> not fulfil the lust of the flesh. (Galatians 5:16)

Remember, victory in the Sprit means death to the flesh. Fasting is a powerful spiritual weapon and a vital weapon in your Christian arsenal.

> For the weapons of our warfare are not carnal,
> but mighty through God to the pulling down of
> strongholds. (2 Corinthians 10:4)

The apostolic warfare algorithm

Algorithm

When it comes time to fight, the Holy Spirit starts unctioning an individual (or church) concerning the need to fast. Fasting instantly ushers you onto the battlefield for a face-to-face showdown with the enemy of your soul. We are told in the third chapter of the book of Hebrews to consider the apostle and high priest of our profession, Christ Jesus. I would like to do just that in this section. I want to share with you about fasting, warfare, and what I call the apostolic algorithm, a technology of the Spirit used by Jesus at the beginning of his ministry. First, I need to lay a foundation from which we will springboard from, the definition of "apostolic," which is a means of or relating to or deriving from the apostles or their teachings. In this case, we are considering the apostle Christ Jesus, the sent one from

God. When you examine the ministry of Jesus, you find that he not only taught his disciples, but he also trained them by his example of doing the works of God. This includes preaching the gospel of the kingdom, healing the sick, casting out demons, opening blind eyes, cleaning the lepers, and raising the dead. Jesus taught it and did it or he taught it and demonstrated it. Even so, today, we, being his disciples, can learn much from his teachings in the scriptures and by examining his actions in performing or demonstrating the works of God. Now let's look at the definition of an algorithm.

An algorithm is a precise step-by-step plan for a computational procedure that begins with an input value and yields an output value in a finite number of steps. It is a precise rule (or set of rules) specifying how to solve some problem.

Note, an algorithm starts with an input value and then yields (creates, makes, or produces) an output value. One of the definitions for the word yield is to give something as a result. It is a transitive verb, which means to produce something as the result of work, activity, or calculation. In this apostolic algorithm, we see this input value.

Input Value

> And Jesus being full of the Holy Ghost returned from Jordan, and was led by the Spirit into the wilderness, being forty days tempted of the devil. And in those days he did eat nothing: and when they were ended, he afterward hungered. (Luke 4:1–2)

Now in the fourteenth verse of the same chapter, we see the algorithms yielded output value.

Output value

> And Jesus returned in the power of the Spirit
> into Galilee: and there went out a fame of him
> through all the region round about. (Luke 4:14)

Jesus went from being full of the Holy Ghost to flowing in the power of the Spirit. An apostolic people are warring people taught (Psalm 144:1) and trained by the Lord of hosts to violently possess (Matthew 11:12) and establish the kingdom of God. As a result, conflict with the enemy is inevitable. In times past, I have seen positive results in spiritual warfare accomplished by my pursuance in praying against enemy strongholds in the heavenlies. I still believe in that approach and basic line of doctrine; however, there is also a battle being waged for the real estate of your soul. This is the real estate of your mind, your will, and your emotions. The above scripture is more in line with that type of warfare we must undertake to walk in the power of the Spirit. The warfare you experience as you fast, pray, and press into the will of the Lord for your life. As we sought and obey the leading of the Holy Spirit in prayer and fasting, many of us were led to our own personal wilderness, where we engage the enemy in spiritual warfare.

I believe this is where the first real battle and victory must be won. We must win this battle just as Jesus did if we expect to walk in authority and power. What do I mean, you ask. Let's look at this technology, the apostolic algorithm that Jesus used. As Jesus was full of the Holy Ghost and was led by the Spirit into the wilderness to be tempted, according to Luke 4:12, the Bible says in John 16:13 that the Holy Spirit will guide us. Guide is the word *hodegeo*, meaning to show the way; to teach you into all truth. The Holy Spirit being the third person of the Godhead has insight that we do not possess, but this wisdom can be downloaded to our spirit and made available for our understanding by the Holy Spirit. The Holy Spirit can take the battle to the enemy the way a slam dunk basketball player takes the ball to the hoop. The apostle Paul said it like this:

> I therefore so run, not as uncertainly; so fight I, not as one that beateth the air: But I keep under my body, and bring it into subjection. (1 Corinthians 9:26–27)

Just as a boxer will work out for an upcoming bout, fasting trains our flesh and soul to "shut up" so we can develop the spiritual accuracy needed to defeat the enemy. Paul put no trust in his flesh; the apostle in essence is saying, "Look, this is a real battle. I'm not shadow boxing nor am I throwing wild haymakers; I'm making every punch count." By disciplining his body (most likely by fasting), he brought it into subjection the Greek word *doulagogeo* (doo-lag-ogue-eh'-o) which means to be a slave driver, to enslave, to subdue, to subject to stern and rigid discipline. Let's face it. If you do not discipline, subdue, or enslave your flesh, it will rise up to subdue and enslave you. The Church today consists of a remnant of apostolic saints that are militant in their praise, fervent in prayer, intimate in their worship, and tenacious in their quest to advance the kingdom in righteousness. They are laying down their lives through fasting so that the reality of the life of Christ can be seen in the earth. The best way to describe it is "hunger," a driving hunger for a deep, intimate relationship with the Lord. This hunger supersedes their appetite for daily bread.

> Neither have I gone back from the commandment of his lips; I have esteemed the words of His mouth more than my necessary food. (Job 23:12)

This profound desire and driving obsession to experience and personify the Son of God (Romans 8:19) expresses itself as a vicious pursuit. Christians all over the world are expanding the kingdom within themselves, their cities, regions, and nations, fasting, praying, pushing, and pressing to possess and manifest the treasure within.

> But we have this treasure in earthen vessels, that
> the excellency of the power may be of God, and
> not of us. (2 Corinthians 4:7)

Plunged into the spirit realm

It is a known fact that people involved in the occult use drugs, hypnoses, animal and human sacrifices, among other wicked means to tap into the spirit realm illegally. However, being born of the Spirit as children of God, walking in the Spirit according to our new divine nature, is our birthright. Nevertheless, our new nature must be developed through faith (2 Peter 1:3–4) that comes from the reading and revelation of the scriptures. Our new nature develops with spiritual maturity and can be tutored and sharpened by training.

> But strong meat belongeth to them that are of
> full age, even those who by reason of use have
> their senses exercised to discern both good and
> evil. (Hebrews 5:14)

The strong meat in the above scripture represents spiritual full discernment or full knowledge of Christ. *Epignosis* is the Greek word used for knowledge in Ephesians 4:12–13. The Christian of full spiritual age is one that has been weaned from the milk of God's word and is able to digest the meat of God's word. This scripture seems to suggest that spiritual maturity can be fast-tracked in those who exercise their spiritual senses. To do this, enroll in the school of the Holy Spirit so he can give you one-on-one training; this, coupled with study of the scriptures, will enable you to discern both what is good and what is evil. To enroll, give yourself to fasting and prayer. Fasting and prayer will thrust you into the realm of the Spirit.

The temptation of Jesus

> And Jesus being full of the Holy Ghost returned from Jordan, and was led by the Spirit into the wilderness, Being forty days tempted of the devil. And in those days he did eat nothing: and when they were ended, he afterward hungered. (Luke 4:1–2)

> Then was Jesus led up of the spirit into the wilderness to be tempted of the devil. And when he had fasted forty days and forty nights, he was afterward an hungred. (Matthew 4:1–2)

The Bible chronicles the temptation or testing of Jesus in these two New Testament books. Here we learn that after forty days and forty nights of fasting ended, Jesus became hungry and was tempted by the devil on three specific fronts: (1) the lust of the flesh, (2) the lust of the eyes, and (3) the pride of life (1 John 2:16). The three recorded temptations of Jesus are indicative to the serpent tempting the woman (Genesis 3:4–6) and mankind's subsequent fall in the garden of Eden.

The account of the temptation of our Lord is given in both Luke and Matthew. Jesus, like Adam (Genesis 3:6), was tested in the three areas of physical appetite, worldly ambition, and spiritual attainment, in order that he might be proved competent for his mission. Where the first man failed, he triumphed (Wycliffe).

The phrase "being forty days tempted of the devil" in Luke has led some theologians to further believe (and I concur) that the three tests recorded both Matthew and Luke occurred after this time period of forty days and nights were complete, but other temptations had also occurred throughout this period according to Luke 4:2.

Traditionally, when we read the accounts of the temptations of Jesus, we may see Him (in our mind's eye) fasting for forty days, and at the end of the fast, Jesus is tempted three times by the devil. Perhaps this is not all that happened within this period of time. The scripture says that the Spirit led him into the wilderness where he was tempted forty days, which leads us to believe that he was not merely tempted three times after forty days, but it appears that he could have at least been tempted once each day or more of the forty days and nights he fasted.

When you start fasting, you're plunged into the spirit realm. In this realm, you will contend with evil. If we have not been thoroughly purged (most of us are not), our challenge will be with the hidden evil (sin) within our own soul or "self-life" (Matthew 16:24–26; Mark 8:34–36; Luke 9:23–25). Unlike us, Jesus did not have this issue of sin. We know this because of his virgin birth, and this is also revealed in John 14:30 when Jesus says, "Hereafter I will not talk much with you: for the prince of this world cometh, and hath nothing in me." What Jesus means is that the enemy had no hold, power, leverage, or sin that he could use against him, but in our fallen state, our battle against the enemy is much different. When sin or evil intent is uncovered within us, we must first repent (1 John 1:9), we then humble our flesh (1 Corinthians 9:27), and our soul or self-life must then be crucified in that area (Galatians 2:20), then the spirit of our mind must be renewed to take on the mindset of the new creature we are in Christ (Ephesians 4:22–24). You may say, "Brother David, I never had to fight like this before. It seems so overwhelming; everything's gone haywire." Welcome to the battle, my friend. This is a battle for the restoration of your soul, and you are the resistance (1 Peter 5:8–9; James 4:7).

> He restoreth my soul: he leadeth me in the paths
> of righteousness for his name's sake. (Psalm 23:3)

The Spirit of God is leading you to challenge and conquer the enemy strongholds in your own life (self-deliverance) so that you can be free, and then be used to set others free. Over the years, I have dealt with many saints with fragmented souls. Portions of their soul had been literally taken over by demonic influence. The sad part about this is that sometimes the demonic entrenchment is so deep and so skillfully woven into what they believe to be their own personality that they cannot detect or recognize the enemy; and they will fight against the truth to maintain their deception.

In most cases, this rejection of truth is subtle but is most strongly evident in schizophrenic and homosexual bondage. However, the clever and less pronounced deceptions within our souls are more numerous than the extremes, and only fasting and prayer can confirm them in light. Can the saints of the Most High God be deceived? This is the wrong question. The question we should ask is, "How deceived are we?" How many times has God used different individuals in the body of Christ to share the same truth with us that we have rejected repeatedly at face value? Oh, I thank God that he is able to restore our souls; nevertheless, he will not force restoration. We must humble ourselves and cooperate with the Holy Spirit in order to experience the restoration of our souls. If we refuse to deny our "self-life" and fleshly appetites, (antinomianism) our souls will never be restored; and we will end up being an enemy of the Lord and an enemy of his body (the Church).

> For many walk, of whom I have told you often, and now tell you even weeping, that they are the enemies of the cross of Christ: Whose end is destruction, whose God is their belly, and whose glory is in their shame, who mind earthly things. (Philippians 3:18–19)

Contemporary English version:

> I often warned you that many people are living as enemies of the cross of Christ. And now with tears in my eyes, I warn you again that they are headed for hell! They worship their stomachs and brag about the disgusting things they do. All they can think about are the things of this world. (Philippians 3:18–19)

Only the truth can make one free, so fast and pray and seek the Spirit of truth to enlighten your understanding. One must want to be free and be willing to do whatever is necessary to obtain it, including self-denial. If one wins the battle here by cooperating with the Holy Spirit, a victorious outcome will be witnessed in the natural realm. I believe that Jesus, during his wilderness experience, was tempted every day, for forty days, perhaps even several times per day; but hallelujah! He never fell to sin.

> For we have not an high priest which cannot be
> touched with the feeling of our infirmities; but
> was in all points tempted like as we are, yet with-
> out sin. (Hebrews 4:15)

Now he is calling us to overcome. In order for the Lord to teach his people to fight, he must lead them into battle with the enemy. In this way, he teaches us warfare.

> Blessed be the LORD my strength which teacheth
> my hands to war, and my fingers to fight. (Psalm
> 144:1)

The Lord cannot teach us warfare unless he brings us face-to-face with the enemies of our soul. So, the Holy Spirit leads us to fast so we can confront the thing that binds, harasses, and torments us. Fasting automatically brings us into confrontation with forces of darkness.

The Spirit-led fast

> Is not this the fast that I have chosen? to loose the
> bands of wickedness, to undo the heavy burdens,
> and to let the oppressed go free, and that ye break
> every yoke? (Isaiah 58:6)

A Spirit-led fast will be by unction of the Holy Spirit. You say, "What do you mean, Brother David?" I mean that the Holy Spirit will start nudging and impressing you with the necessity to fast. In personal or corporate fasting, the Spirit will most always impress you with the length and type of fast. The fast chosen and honored by the Lord will impact four major areas. Below are the results of fasting:

Loose the bands of wickedness. There are some people that are bound by bands of wickedness; the enemy has them wrapped up, tied up with bands of wickedness—this includes the unregenerate and those that are born again, saints that have a genuine call of God on their lives but because the enemy has bands on them, they seem to never be able to remain free. They are up and down, in and out. I believe that curses function with bands and cords of wickedness. Scripture teaches that fasting breaks these bands. These bands can also be the results of unconfessed sin.

> His own iniquities shall take the wicked himself,
> and he shall be holden with the cords of his sins.
> (Proverbs 5:22)

This word *wicked* means "morally wrong"; do not mistake it to mean "unsaved." When we fast for the lost or the backslider, we bind the power of darkness over their lives, giving that individual the opportunity to exercise his or her will to make a quality decision toward salvation or holiness.

Undo the heavy burdens. There are people that are so weighed down by the enemy that they have become hopeless. When you are around them, you can sense a drag on your spirit. Their lives seem to have no joy or peace because the enemy has placed such heavy loads on the shoulders of their souls. Their life has no meaning or purpose; suicide seems their only escape.

The oppressed go free. Many are so oppressed that only fasting, prayer, and revelation can release the shackles and break the emotional atmospheres of bondage and spiritual death. This is particularly true of people bound by the spirit of witchcraft. Years ago, when God started using me in the ministry of deliverance (the casting out of unclean spirits [Mark 16:17]), my wife and I would drive the streets to find drunkards and homeless people. Then we would bring them to our home, wash their clothes, feed them, preach the gospel, and cast devils out of them all in the same day. The people I ministered to knew little to nothing about church and had no church home; so I started sending them to churches around the city, and God rebuked me and said, "I sent them to you… You teach them." I was reluctant, but I obeyed. I started a Bible study in my wife's beauty salon because many of the people had gotten saved and or ministered to in that building. I had faith to believe that what God said in his word was true, so I taught it, and God moved, setting people free in that beauty salon, and the word got out.

People from other churches started sneaking to our Bible study for deliverance because their pastor did not believe in it. To make a long story short, one day, a woman from a major denomination and one of the largest churches in the city came to our Bible study to spy us out. She was from the church that my wife formerly belonged to and word had gotten back to the pastor that some of his members had come. This woman stood up and said, "It's not right what you are doing here! I am going to tell my pastor and we are going to put you on the altar." I didn't really know what she meant, nor did I know that I was in deep trouble.

About a week later, we got a strange letter in our mailbox. The envelope was filled with some sort of sand or powder mixed with what appeared to be strands of hair, bones, and glass. The letter was on white typing paper with letters cut out of a magazine pasted to it, which I did not read. We knew it was witchcraft, and when several other similar letters arrived, we trashed them. I, like most people, had heard about witchcraft when I was growing up. It was something we laughed and joked about. It was something you see in movies, but in real life I didn't believe it was true. Soon after the letters, a spirit of oppression which I could not shake hit me. I had always been able to motivate myself, but nothing was working. I would go to bed and wake up listless and exhausted. At lunchtime, I would go home and nap, but I never could get enough rest. The joy of life had left me, and as I went about my day, it seemed that I was just going through the motions. I literally felt like a walking dead man. The only difference between me and a dead person was that I had not yet been buried, but I felt dead and was growing more and more weary day after day. I went to the doctor, but he could find nothing wrong with me. He prescribed muscle relaxers, but they didn't help. I would wake up at night gripped with fear, paralyzed from head to foot with a weight sitting on my body, unable to move anything more than my lips whispering, "Jesus! Help me!" And the weight would lift, and strength returned to my limbs.

Several months had gone by, and I was not getting any better. I went to other ministers, but none could help, and some did not want to hear about demons or devils, much less witchcraft. They were afraid and started avoiding me. My doctor began to think I had mental problems. Then I diligently sought the Lord, fasting and praying, spending my entire weekends in our walk-in closet, crying out to God and searching the scriptures. Several more months passed; and then one day while reading the Bible in the book of Psalms, the words on the page seemed to come alive. "Yea, though I walk through the valley of the shadow of death."

Instantly, I knew that I was in this valley, and death was shadowing me. The only difference between me and a dead person was that I had not yet been buried; but I was growing very weary. I was tired of fighting, and I was losing strength. Let me go on record saying, "The valley of the shadow of death is a real place; I have been there." This revelation was the only *rhema* I had experienced in many months of constant fasting and prayer. As tears filled my eyes and ran down my cheeks, I knew that the Lord was speaking to me. I believed in my heart that God was greater than death. I knew he had raised Jesus from the dead, and I saw with the eyes of my spirit he could raise me up also. I knew I was under attack and knew I had to use my faith and spiritual authority against this force of darkness that was stalking me. As I turned around to confront and look the shadow of death in the eyes, and speak the word of faith in my heart, my strength and will to fight collapsed. I fell to my face on my bathroom floor surrounded by the hosts of hell. As I looked around, I began slipping into a deep sense of hopelessness, not knowing what the will of the Lord was.

I saw that I was well outnumbered; there were too many of them. I couldn't seem to muster the power to fight. Lying there, I could feel the life being sucked from my soul. I knew within myself that I had only enough strength to make one final cry of supplication to the Lord. Quietly I whispered, "Lord, if you want me to die here, I surrender. I know you can raise me from the dead. So let's get this over with; I am tired of fighting; but if you deliver me, I will go any- where you send me and I will say whatever you tell me to say."

Suddenly, the oppression lifted, and life started to flow back into my soul; my spirit was refreshed, and the Lord spoke these words:

> "I have allowed this bondage to come on you
> so that you can know that it [witchcraft] is real
> and so you can have compassion for my people.
> Many are bound but few believe their bondage;
> many are bound and there are few that help."

Break the yoke. Fasting seems to strengthen our faith. It gives us an expectancy that supersedes our natural perspective and short-cir- cuits unbelief. Fasting brings an anointing to break yokes in other people's lives. You must pay a price to set other people free, the price of fasting and prayer. You fast so that others can be freed. The Lord wants us to break every yoke. Some yokes will not be broken unless we fast and cry out to God in prayer. The Lord instructs his leaders to blow the trumpet in Zion, summon everyone, sanctify a fast, and call a solemn assembly (Joel 2:15–17) in hope of divine mercy. The outpouring of God's spirit comes after we fast, not before.

> And it shall come to pass afterward that I will
> pour out My Spirit on all flesh; Your sons and
> our daughters shall prophesy; Your old men shall

dream dreams; Your young men shall see visions. (Joel 2:28)

This move of God is the result of what took place prior to the outpouring. As I said earlier, a price must be paid, but understand that we are not paying God to pour out his spirit or for the anointing; however, we are positioning ourselves to receive.

> Therefore also now, saith the LORD, turn ye even to me with all your heart, and with fasting, and with weeping, and with mourning: And rend your heart, and not your garments, and turn unto the LORD your God: for he is gracious and merciful, slow to anger, and of great kindness, and repenteth him of the evil. (Joel 2:12–13)

Fast that I have chosen

> Is not this the fast that I have chosen? To loose the bands of wickedness, to undo the heavy burdens, and to let the oppressed go free, and that ye break every yoke? Is it not to deal thy bread to the hungry, and that thou bring the poor that are cast out to thy house? When thou seest the naked, that thou cover him; and that thou hide not thyself from thine own flesh? Then shall thy light break forth as the morning, and thine health shall spring forth speedily: and thy righteousness shall go before thee; the glory of the LORD shall be thy rereward. Then shalt thou call, and the LORD shall answer; thou shalt cry, and he shall say, Here I am. If thou take away from the midst of thee the yoke, the putting forth of the finger, and speaking vanity; And if thou draw out thy soul to the hungry, and satisfy the afflicted soul; then

shall thy light rise in obscurity, and thy darkness be as the noon day: And the LORD shall guide thee continually, and satisfy thy soul in drought, and make fat thy bones: and thou shalt be like a watered garden, and like a spring of water, whose waters fail not. And they that shall be of thee shall build the old waste places: thou shalt raise up the foundations of many generations; and thou shalt be called, The repairer of the breach, The restorer of paths to dwell in. (Isaiah 58:6–12)

9

Daniel's Twenty-One-Day Fast

As introduction to this section, I would like to take great care and respect in first recognizing the enormity and significance of the book of Daniel in the divine plan of God for his chosen people, the Jews and Christians alike. Entire books have been written, and even more could be written on this one subject alone; yet my scope will be less than exhaustive, focusing mainly on the prophet Daniel and spiritual technologies of faith, prayer, and fasting that can be gleaned from this text. However, from a theological standpoint, it seemed good to me to acknowledge the key theme of this great prophetic, apocalyptic book.

Daniel, like Moses, was an intercessor. It must be understood that Daniel's prayer and fasting was a providential means of accomplishing what God had already determined. This is an important point for us to understand concerning Daniel and his actions after he discerned the will of God. Even when Daniel knew that the end of captivity for his people had arrived, according to the will of God, he was not slack concerning this promise. Daniel pressed his way with prayer and fasting, plus he also integrated additional input algorithms in his pursuit of establishing the will of God. He engaged the enemy in spiritual warfare, coming against the forces of darkness, opening up the heavens, so that the will of God could be accomplished on earth. Even so today, when we discern the will of God, we cannot sit back passively; we must get in the battle. There will be resistance in the heavens, but as kings of the KING of kings, we must rise up as Daniel did and take it by force (Matthew 11:12).

Daniel, as an Old Testament prophet, and apostolic type, moved strongly in what is now commonly referred to as the gifts of the Spirit—prophecy, visions, and dreams. According to scripture, he was a man with an "excellent spirit" (Daniel 5:12) and an unfailing prayer life (Daniel 6:10), earmarked by a tremendous faith which God honored with special miracles (Daniel 3:18–25, 6:20–23).

The technology of consecration

> But Daniel purposed in his heart that he would not defile himself with the portion of the king's meat, nor with the wine which he drank: therefore he requested of the prince of the eunuchs that he might not defile himself. (Daniel 1:8)

When Daniel determined in his heart to set himself apart (by fasting the king's meat and wine), consecrating himself and his apostolic team (Hananiah, Mishael, and Azariah) to God, he triggered something in the glory realm; in only ten days, a tangible physical manifestation of grace could be seen upon their faces.

> And at the end of ten days their countenances appeared fairer and fatter in flesh than all the children which did eat the portion of the king's meat. (Daniel 1:15)

This release of grace in their lives was not confined to their physical bodies but also affected them spiritually, giving them supernatural abilities above and beyond their peers.

> As for these four children, God gave them knowledge and skill in all learning and wisdom: and Daniel had understanding in all visions and

dreams. Now at the end of the days that the king had said he should bring them in, then the prince of the eunuchs brought them in before Nebuchadnezzar. And the king communed with them; and among them all was found none like Daniel, Hananiah, Mishael, and Azariah: therefore stood they before the king. And in all matters of wisdom and understanding, that the king enquired of them, he found them ten times better than all the magicians and astrologers that were in all his realm. (Daniel 1:17–20)

Historical discernment

In the first year of Darius the son of Ahasuerus, of the seed of the Medes, which was made king over the realm of the Chaldeans; In the first year of his reign I Daniel understood by books the number of the years, whereof the word of the LORD came to Jeremiah the prophet, that he would accomplish seventy years in the desolations of Jerusalem. (Daniel 9:1–2)

In these two verses, we see a historical landmark that seemed to stir Daniel's spirit. It was in the first year that king Darius was in office as Daniel studied the Word (scrolls of Jeremiah). He discerned and received revelation that the years of devastation caused by the sins of God's people were about to end.

Daniel's twenty-one-day fast technology

And I set my face unto the Lord God, to seek by prayer and supplications, with fasting, and sackcloth, and ashes. (Daniel 9:3)

Let me give again the definition of an algorithm. An algorithm is a precise step-by-step plan for a computational procedure that begins with an input value and yields an output value in a finite number of steps. It is a precise rule (or set of rules) specifying how to solve some problem.

Algorithm input values:

- Set face to the Lord
- Seek by prayer
- Supplication
- Fasting
- Sackcloth
- Ashes

When God gave Daniel the understanding of the word he was reading in the book of Jeremiah, it provoked him to seek the Lord more intensely. Daniel not only coupled fasting with his already-disciplined prayer life; he also input a set of additional algorithms. Let's take a closer look at these input values.

1. Set his face, positioned his heart and spirit in a continual gaze toward God.
2. Prayer; positioned himself as an intercessor for the nation of Israel.
3. Supplication; took a humble posture with an earnest request petitioning and begging on bended knees.
4. Fasting; humbled his soul with fasting.
5. Sackcloth; an outward manifestation of an inward spiritual reality. Sackcloth is symbolic of a heart in mourning.
6. Ashes; an outward manifestation of an inward spiritual reality. Ashes are the symbol of a repenting heart.

From the book of Daniel (6:4–20), Daniel stands in the gap as intercessor, praying to God, confessing his sins and the sins of his people, the nation of Israel. We can take Daniel's prayer as a model of intercession before God. Look at some of the key elements in Daniel's prayer in light of the New Testament.

1. Daniel's prayer was persistent (Luke 18:6).
2. He had determination (Luke 9:51).
3. He was importunate (Luke 11:8-39).
4. He showed humility (Luke 18:10–14).
5. He made confession (James 5:16).
6. He engaged in petition and intercession (Philippians 4:6).

> And whiles I was speaking, and praying, and confessing my sin and the sin of my people Israel, and presenting my supplication before the LORD my God for the holy mountain of my God; Yea, whiles I was speaking in prayer, even the man Gabriel, whom I had seen in the vision at the beginning, being caused to fly swiftly, touched me about the time of the evening oblation. And he informed me, and talked with me, and said, O Daniel, I am now come forth to give thee skill and understanding. (Daniel 9:20–22)

Twice, Daniel says, "whiles I was speaking and praying and whiles I was speaking in prayer." Daniel was speaking and praying the word, and it caused something to happen in the heavenlies. Wars and battles must be won in the heavens before we see the victory in the natural physical realm. Our fight is not a flesh fight won with money, bullets, and guns, but rather fought in the realm of the spirit (2 Corinthians 10:4). Having read this passage of scripture many times before, I was familiar with this story; but the Holy Spirit unctioned me to read and study it again. When I did, I saw something that I had never seen before.

> Yea, whiles I was speaking in prayer, even the man Gabriel, whom I had seen in the vision

at the beginning, being caused to fly swiftly, touched me about the time of the evening oblation. (Daniel 9:21)

Daniel saw in the spirit the angelic being named Gabriel begin to move (being *caused* to fly swiftly). Daniel was giving "voice" to God's word; as a result, the angel excelled in strength and moved rapidly through the glory realm.

> Bless the LORD, ye his angels, that excel in strength, that do his commandments, hearkening unto the voice of his word. (Psalm 103:20)

Star wars

God's word is written; however, when we read it aloud, we give "voice" to it; and this causes angels to excel in strength. Praying God's word accelerates the movement of angelic beings in the heavenlies. I believe this acceleration was also fueled by the fact that Daniel knew and was praying the will of God concerning the conclusion of the years of captivity for his people. He gave "voice" to what was written; he gave "voice" to the will of God. Angels are always listening to what we say; they are listening for the Word of God spoken in faith that they may execute his will. They are waiting on us to give "voice" to his word and give "voice" to his will so that they can labor on our behalf.

> Are they not all ministering spirits, sent forth to minister for them who shall be heirs of salvation? (Hebrews 1:14)

I like the words "sent forth"; they do my heart good. I think of angels as fighter jets in the spirit realm. During 9/11 attack on the twin towers in New York City, I was living in Illinois, and I saw F16 fighter jets scrambled over Chicago, protecting the Sears Tower.

Sometimes, when troops run into strongholds on the ground, they radio for air support from fighter jets. Fighter jets are awesome birds of prey that can fly faster than the speed of sound, and when mobilized, they can be on point within moments to take out enemy targets or protect ground troops with air support. Angels, on the other hand, travel at the speed of light, 186,000 plus miles per second. That's what I call air superiority!

This happened to me once while ministering in Africa. My team and I left Zambia traveling by land rover headed to Mozambique; however, when we got to the Zambezi Bridge to cross the river, we could not cross because a civil war was going on, large rocks and boulders had been placed on the bridge, and large trucks had been turned over and burned to block crossing. Some on my team were fearful and said, "We must go back. It is too dangerous; they are fighting here." I started praying in the spirit, and I sensed that it was God's will for me to preach in Mozambique; but that bridge was our only way into the country, and I needed that bridge cleared so we could cross. As we waited, my team became more fearful when they understood that I was not turning back.

We went into a small shop where I was able to find a phone that worked; there were no cell phones as we have today, so I placed a collect call to the United States to the pastor of our home church in Chicago. Our time zone was eight hours ahead of Chicago, but thank God my pastor answered the phone. He had been up unable to sleep and immediately asked, "David, what is wrong?" I told him that we needed air support because there was civil war with heavy fighting on the ground, the bridge was blocked, and that I must preach in Mozambique. I told him I needed our intercessory team to go to God on our behalf. He said he would phone the intercessors, and they would start to pray immediately. Two, then three hours went by and nothing seemed to be happening, but I was determined not to turn back and continued to pray in the spirit. Then suddenly, we saw a military convoy approaching the bridge. They were United Nation troops, and when the people saw them, they began to cheer. After another three and one-half hours, the troops secured and cleared the bridge, and we were able to cross safely.

When we reached the church in Mozambique, we found that it had been hit by a spirit of witchcraft; and there were only a handful of saints left after the church split. The pastor and his wife were severely depressed and discouraged and were making plans to leave the area that week. I called for a meeting at the pastor's home. Under a strong apostolic anointing, we were able to minister deliverance to the elders and remaining saints; we broke curses over the church, prophesied restoration, and with the laying on of hands, imparted spiritual gifts to the pastor. One year later, this church had grown to nearly one hundred strong, praise God! To God I give all the glory!

> Yea, whiles I was speaking in prayer, even the man Gabriel, whom I had seen in the vision at the beginning, being caused to fly swiftly, touched me about the time of the evening oblation. (Daniel 9:21)

The word *swiftly* in Greek and Hebrew is *yeaph* which means "to be fatigued or utterly exhausted." This word *yeaph* is from the word *yaaph,* which means "to tire as if from a wearisome fight." While Daniel prayed and fasted, he was allowed to see into the spirit realm. He viewed a battle (star wars) in the sky. This is the real star wars between the angelic host under the leadership of Michael, one of the chief princes and the fallen angelic beings of Satan. There are only two other individuals in the Bible who ever witnessed such events. The apostle John in the book of Revelation gives us a look at the first stellar battle.

> And there was war in heaven: Michael and his angels fought against the dragon; and the dragon fought and his angels, And prevailed not; neither was their place found any more in heaven. (Revelation 12:7–8)

Jesus gives us a concluding view of this battle.

> And he [Jesus] said unto them, I beheld Satan as
> lightning fall from heaven. (Luke 10:18)

From Daniel's witness, it seems that fasting, linked with praying, giving "voice" to God's word, could be the catalyst causing hyperacceleration (warp drive) in the glory realm. Angels not only execute the will of God but they *excel in strength* doing it at *warp drive speed*—rapidly, immediately, without delay. "Beam me up, Scottie!" If we use the Greek words to describe this celestial activity, we could say that the angel Gabriel was literally exhausted from fighting and soaring so rapidly. Now you have to understand that Gabriel was no ordinary angel; he was a messenger, and his home was the throne room of God. He actually stood in God's presence (Luke 1:19); that's powerful! He had to be soaked with God's glory! However, the principality over Persia outranked him.

Principality, or in Greek, *archas* means chief ruler or being of the highest ranking in Satan's kingdom. Principality is the territory, position, or jurisdiction of a prince; sovereignty. Powers or *exousias* means authorities, those who derive their power from and execute the will of the principalities or chief ruler. Princes or chief rulers can rule over countries, states, cities, religious denominations, neighborhoods, political parties, ethnic groups, etc. A prince is a fallen angel with a celestial (heavenly) body dwelling in the heavens.

> There are also celestial bodies, and bodies terrestrial: but the glory of the celestial is one and the glory of the terrestrial is another. (1 Corinthians 15:40)

In the King James Version of the Bible, demons, referred to as devils or unclean spirits, are actually disembodied spirits that need human bodies to fully express their wickedness. Above every demon or demon group is a prince (fallen angel) who rules a principality (location or jurisdiction). A prince will not indwell a terrestrial (earth dwelling) body as it would restrict the sphere of his power and influ-ence. Demons, however, crave the terrestrial body and consider it their home (Luke 11:24).

> In the third year of Cyrus king of Persia a thing was revealed unto Daniel, whose name was called Belteshazzar; and the thing was true, but the time appointed was long: and he understood the thing, and had understanding of the vision. In those days I Daniel was mourning three full weeks. I ate no pleasant bread, neither came flesh nor wine in my mouth, neither did I anoint myself at all, till three whole weeks were fulfilled. (Daniel 10:1–3)

> Then said he unto me, Fear not, Daniel: for from the first day that thou didst set thine heart to understand, and to chasten thyself before thy God, thy words were heard, and I am come for thy words. (Daniel 10:12)

When we seek the Lord and pray, our words are heard immedi-ately in the throne room of glory. It would seem that this scripture is teaching that when we pray God hears the voice of his Word that we speak on earth; then in heaven, he releases or sends forth a response. Notice: Gabriel came because of Daniel's words.

> So shall my word be that goeth forth out of my mouth: it shall not return unto me void, but it shall accomplish that which I please, and it shall prosper in the thing whereto I sent it. (Isaiah 55:11)

Before the angel gives Daniel the answer to his prayer, he vol-untary begins to give insight into the workings of the spirit realm that had he not, there would be no way we could have known. Keep in mind that Daniel did not have the promise written in Matthew 16:19 ("And I will give unto thee the keys of the kingdom of heaven: and whatsoever thou shalt bind on earth shall be bound in heaven: and whatsoever thou shalt loose on earth shall be loosed in heaven"). Nevertheless, major warfare is being waged in the heavens as Daniel fasted, prayed, and wrestled with spiritual wickedness in high places.

> But the prince of the kingdom of Persia withstood me one and twenty days: but, lo, Michael, one of the chief princes, came to help me; and I remained there with the kings of Persia. (Daniel 10:13)

> In those days I Daniel was mourning three full weeks I ate no pleasant bread, neither came flesh nor wine in my mouth, neither did I anoint myself at all, till three whole weeks were fulfilled. (Daniel 10:2–3)

No matter how you look at it, *three full weeks* or *three whole weeks* both add up to the number of days the angel said he was hindered before being able to break free with the help of Michael, one of the chief princes.

> But the prince of the kingdom of Persia withstood me one and twenty days. (Daniel 10:13)

According to the testimony of the angel Gabriel, it was on the twenty-first day that Daniel got a breakthrough in prayer; but according to Daniel's account, he didn't receive the actual manifestation of visitation from the Lord until the twenty-fourth day. Even at warp speed, it took three additional days.

> And in the four and twentieth day of the first month, as I was by the side of the great river, which is Hiddekel; Then I lifted up mine eyes,

and looked, and behold a certain man clothed in linen, whose loins were girded with fine gold of Uphaz: His body also was like the beryl, and his face as the appearance of lightning, and his eyes as lamps of fire, and his arms and his feet like in colour to polished brass, and the voice of his words like the voice of a multitude. (Daniel 10:4–6).

Twenty-one breakthrough

Daniel was a breakthrough believer. He made up his mind that he had to have a breakthrough, so he added fasting with his prayer in seeking the Lord on behalf of his will for his people. Other than this account in the book of Daniel, there seems to be no biblical account connecting fasting and the numeral twenty-one. I ask the question: Could the number twenty-one stand for breakthrough? According to scripture, it was on the twenty-first day of Daniel's fast that the angel Gabriel was able to break free from the prince of Persia after receiving help from the chief prince, Michael. We know from this description that Daniel was in a high-altitude battle, not hand-to-hand combat; this battle raged in the heavens. However, the thing that should strike us most about this account is that even though God had answered his prayer the first day he prayed, there was still opposition and hindrance in the spirit realm trying to stop God's answer to prayer from ever reaching him. Daniel made up his mind that he *had to have a breakthrough*. He set his face to seek the Lord with prayer *and fasting*, wrestling against the forces of darkness until the victory was won.

There comes a time in every Christian's life where he refuses to be content with the mundane and normal. He refuses to be satisfied by the carnal pleasures of his physical life. There comes a cry, a craving, a hunger, a thirst from deep within which cannot be quenched by the dainties of natural nourishment. It is a cry to look upon, to see the face, the hand, and glory of God.

> And he said, I beseech thee, shew me thy glory. And he said, I will make all my goodness pass before thee, and I will proclaim the name of the LORD before thee; and will be gracious to whom I will be gracious, and will shew mercy on whom I will shew mercy. And he said, Thou canst not see my face: for there shall no man see me, and live. And the LORD said, Behold, there is a place by me, and thou shalt stand upon a rock: And it shall come to pass, while my glory passeth by, that I will put thee in a clift of the rock, and will cover thee with my hand while I pass by: And I will take away mine hand, and thou shalt see my back parts: but my face shall not be seen. (Exodus 33:18–23)

Are you in a battle looking for the hand and goodness of God? That place of glory can be accessed from within; it is Christ in you, the hope of glory. Don't give up, don't cave in, and *do not quit!* Keep fasting and keep praying and giving "voice" to His word.

> For we wrestle not against flesh and blood, but against principalities, against powers, against the rulers of the darkness of this world, against spiritual wickedness in high places. (Ephesians 6:12)

We (the church) are taking the battle to the enemy with a holy anger, claiming our inheritance in the kingdom of God. Being led by the Holy Spirit in fasting and prayer, we will confront the enemy and take the kingdom by force!

> And from the days of John the Baptist until now the kingdom of heaven suffereth violence, and the violent take it by force. (Matthew 11:12)

Rewards of fasting

1. The Lord promises to restore fellowship, intimate communion, blessing, and divine health to those who fast and abandon hypocrisy (two-facedness) and stop making (false) accusation of the innocent.
2. The Lord promises that your present state of darkness, calamity, and distress shall be replaced by the sunshine of his favor and guidance, plus immunity to recession and drought.
3. The Lord promises that your life will be a source of refreshment, a flow of godly influence, while sharing your blessings with others.
4. The Lord promises to use you to repair the decay of moral foundations and restore honor, respect, and godly character as a way of life.
5. The Lord promises that if you respect his Sabbath and keep it holy, he will cause you to ride on the high places and feed you the heritage of Jacob. This means spiritual exaltation and divine prosperity.

Read the promise in the book of Isaiah:

> Then shall thy light break forth as the morning, and thine health shall spring forth speedily: and thy righteousness shall go before thee; the glory of the LORD shall be thy rereward. Then shalt thou call, and the LORD shall answer; thou shalt cry, and he shall say, Here I am. If thou take away from the midst of thee the yoke, the putting forth of the finger, and speaking vanity; And if thou draw out thy soul to the hungry, and satisfy the afflicted soul; then shall thy light rise in obscurity, and thy darkness be as the noon day: And the LORD shall guide thee continually, and satisfy thy soul in drought, and make fat thy

bones: and thou shalt be like a watered garden, and like a spring of water, whose waters fail not. And they that shall be of thee shall build the old waste places: thou shalt raise up the foundations of many generations; and thou shalt be called, The repairer of the breach, The restorer of paths to dwell in. If thou turn away thy foot from the sabbath, from doing thy pleasure on my holy day; and call the sabbath a delight, the holy of the LORD, honourable; and shalt honour him, not doing thine own ways, nor finding thine own pleasure, nor speaking thine own words: Then shalt thou delight thyself in the LORD; and I will cause thee to ride upon the high places of the earth, and feed thee with the heritage of Jacob thy father: for the mouth of the LORD hath spoken it. (Isaiah 58:8–14)

Notes

1   Dennis H. McCallum, "Watchman Nee and the House Church Movement" (1986), http://www.xenos.org/essays/neeframe.htm

2   Bill Schiller, "Christians come under attack in China," Toronto Star (2010), http://www.thestar.com/news/world/china/article/845270-christians-come-under-attack-in-china

3   "Constantine the Great," Wikipedia, https://en.wikipedia.org/wiki/Constantine _the_Great

4   18 Jan. 2911 http://www.wordiq.com/definition/Demobilization

5   Strongs 5179 tupos

6   Strongs 6754 tselem

7   Strongs 0342 eybah

8   Strongs 7218 ro'sh

9   Strongs 6119 `aqeb

10 Drea Knufken, "20 Animals That Have Been Cloned," Business Pundit (2009), http://www.businesspundit.com/20-animals-that-have-been-cloned

11 Wikipediafreeencyclopedia

12 From Wikipedia, the free encyclopedia

13 Neil Cole, "Organic Church" (2010): 109–121, http://www.cmaresources.org/article/dna

14 Strongs 4151

15 Strongs2233

16 Strongs 1411

17 Strongs 5310

18 Strongs 1982

19 Matt Slick, "Jesus' Two Natures: God and Man," Christian Apologetics & Research Ministry (2008), http://carm.org/jesus-two-natures

20 Strongs 0536

21 Strongs 1484

22 Strongs 5481

23 "Reform," Merriam-Webster, www.merriamwebster.com

24 "Reform," http://1828.mshaffer.com/d/search/word,reform

25 Geoffrey William Bromiley, Theological Dictionary of the New Testament Volume 1, 74 By Geoffrey William Bromiley page 74

26 Geoffrey William Bromiley, Theological Dictionary of the New Testament Volume 1, 72

27 Geoffrey William Bromiley, Theological Dictionary of the New Testament Volume 1, 188

28 "Why was Azusa street revival so Dynamic" by Basie Martins. March 21, 2021. https://www.asrmartins.com/why-was-the-azusa-street-revival-so-dynamic/.

29 Wikipedia Encyclopedia

30 Christine L. Case. "Handwashing." Access: Excellence. www.accessexcellence. org/.

31 Wikipedia the free encyclopedia

32 https://www.bibleevidences.com/medical-evidence/

33 https://www.bibleevidences.com/medical-evidence/

34 Med-Planet encyclopedia

35 Ruth Heflin, Glory Experiencing the Atmosphere of Heaven (McDougal Publishing, 1996) page 11. Kindle edition.

36 Word at Work July, 2010. Word at Work Ministries Permission to quote Al Houghton.
   1. Introduction Page 1. 2. WEDNESDAY, JULY 7 Scripture: Leviticus 16:6-10 page 4. 3. MONDAY, JULY 12 Scripture: 1 Kings 3:19-28 page 5. 4. TUESDAY, JULY 13 Scripture: Psalm 2:1-6 page 6. 5. WEDNESDAY, JULY 14 Scripture: Psalm 2:7-12 page 6. 6. FRIDAY, JULY 23 Scripture: Romans 13:1-4 page 8-9

37 Eckhart Tolle, The Power of Now (1997)

38 Watchman Nee, The Spiritual Man (1928)

About the Author

David Stafford currently oversees Kingdom Fellowship International, counseling leaders and disciplining families in kingdom truths for covenant relationships. He is owner and functions as general manager of For His Kingdom (Global) Radio (FHKR), www.forhiskingdomradio.com, David Stafford Ministries (DSM), Do the Word Publishing, and as the host and executive producer of Do the Word radio broadcast spreading the Gospel of the kingdom.

David ministers in a methodical revelatory teaching grace and strong deliverance anointing that sets people free. He is known as a risk-taker, a man of prayer with an uncompromising word and a cutting-edge kingdom message. His passion is to perfect the saints (Ephesians 4:12). The calling on his life led him on mission trips to several nations in Africa, including Zambia, Mozambique, and Malawi with church plants in Lilongwe, Malawi, and Blantyre.

In the late '80s and early '90s, he was used by God to help pioneer the message of deliverance. Along with the late Evangelist Melvin L. Smith Sr. David also ministered and taught spiritual warfare and training deliverance teams in Jackson, Mississippi, and in Chicago, Illinois, with Apostle John Eckhardt at Crusaders Church of God in Christ. David has four children: David, Deanna, Donald, and Grace. He is married to Jacquelyn Stafford, a virtuous godly woman. He and his wife, Jacquelyn, currently reside in the Dallas-Fort Worth metroplex.